YVES CONGAR

MODERN SPIRITUAL MASTERS SERIES

YVES CONGAR

Essential Writings

Selected with an Introduction by

PAUL LAKELAND

ORBIS BOOKS
Maryknoll, New York 10545

Founded in 1970, Orbis Books endeavors to publish works that enlighten the mind, nourish the spirit, and challenge the conscience. The publishing arm of the Maryknoll Fathers and Brothers, Orbis seeks to explore the global dimensions of the Christian faith and mission, to invite dialogue with diverse cultures and religious traditions, and to serve the cause of reconciliation and peace. The books published reflect the views of their authors and do not represent the official position of the Maryknoll Society. To learn more about Maryknoll and Orbis Books, please visit our website at www.maryknollsociety.org.

Published by Orbis Books, Maryknoll, NY 10545-0302.

Queries regarding rights and permissions should be addressed to:
Orbis Books, P.O. Box 302, Maryknoll, NY 10545-0302.

Manufactured in the United States of America.

Library of Congress Cataloging-in-Publication Data

Congar, Yves, 1904–1995.
[Selections. English. 2010]
Essential writings / Yves Congar ; selected with an introduction by Paul Lakeland.
p. cm. – (Modern spiritual masters series)
ISBN 978-1-57075-787-7 (pbk.)
1. Theology. 2. Catholic Church – Doctrines. I. Lakeland, Paul, 1946– II. Title.
BX4705.C76A25 2010
230'.2 – dc22 2009034386

Contents

Preface 7

Sources 11

Introduction 13

1. CONGAR THE ECUMENIST 37

2. CONGAR THE ECCLESIOLOGIST 56

3. CONGAR AND THE LAITY 80

4. CONGAR AND THE SPIRITUAL LIFE 124

On the Holy Angels 124
St. Peter 129
St. Thomas Aquinas: Servant of the Truth 135
Christmas Is, First of All, Jesus Christ 150
The Three Ages of the Spiritual Life 152
The Youthful Heart 165

5. CONGAR AND THE HOLY SPIRIT 175

Life in the Church: Teaching 192
Sacramental Life and Sanctification 196
The Life of the Church as a Society and Its Spiritual Government 197

Preface

To fall in love with a dead person is a trying experience. There is something quite uncanny about giving your heart to someone literally unattainable, and yet the emotions seem just as real as if he or she were standing before you. This was my experience encountering the work of Yves Congar, the Dominican friar and theologian from whose capacious writings some few selections are gathered in this present volume. Congar from his photographs was no movie star, and from the testimony of those who knew him best, by no means easy to get along with. Indeed, when my heart was moved by Congar, I hadn't even seen a picture of him, and when my eyes eventually lighted on the elderly features of the friar at his desk, looking like a rather frazzled Tom Merton, it did nothing for me at all. But neither did it cause me to lose any of my personal fascination with this remarkable man, and the book before you is at least partly my homage to someone I wish I had been privileged to know, someone to whom all contemporary Roman Catholics owe far more than they could possibly know, and someone whose life in many ways recapitulates the fortunes of the twentieth-century Catholic Church.

I came to Congar when in the year 2000 I began to think that theological reflection on the laity was sorely underdeveloped and that I would like to write a book to help fill the gap. Even Vatican II, though it had placed the lay apostolate front and center, seemed to shy away from asking the question "What exactly *is* a layperson?" Perhaps it was because you cannot ask that question without finding yourself asking the bigger one, "What, then, is the Church?" At any rate, when anyone looks back at the corpus of twentieth-century theology, there is one colossus of a book on the theology of the laity, Congar's *Laypeople in the Church,* written around 1950 and revised during Vatican II some twelve years later. Congar was a Dominican friar, a person raised and trained in very traditional circles, but the openness of his approach to ecclesial realities is evident. It seems to come on the one hand from the inner freedom that only a life of deep personal prayer can produce and, on the other, out of an unparalleled knowledge of the writings from the first centuries of the Christian era. Together, these were an explosive combination, and they excited and energized me when I encountered them. What follows here is tribute to the man who inspired my own poor efforts at a theology of the laity in my 2003 book, *The Liberation of the Laity: In Search of an Accountable Church.* I do not know if he would have liked the book. But in any case, as they say, I owe it all to him.

The writings of Congar gathered in this book are selected from the over two thousand items in his personal bibliography. The principle of selection from so much material requires a word of explanation. Theologians and historians of the Catholic Church are well acquainted with the work of Congar and do not need this kind of sampling of his ideas. This book is not primarily directed at them, though even they may find some surprising material here. Rather, it reaches out to students and others who may or may not have heard the name of Yves Congar, but who could benefit from seeing how the ideas of one man shaped so much of the postconciliar Church and, indeed, how fresh and important these ideas remain today. Congar's many books included large, scholarly works, most of which remain in print in his native French, English, and other languages. Here the reader will find extracts from some of them. But he also published collections of shorter pieces, most of them translated into English. These often more accessible essays are now mostly long out of print, but many of them are excerpted in the following pages. And then there are the countless essays and one or two books that never were translated into English, and that consequently few people who do not read French have encountered. These too are present in what follows. But the overall objective is not so much to provide previously or currently inaccessible writing samples as to offer a portrait of the work of a man of enormous learning, influence, and personal simplicity, for those who might otherwise not have the chance to encounter him. Who knows, you too might fall in love with him!

Just as I have selected samples of Congar's writings whose style reflects his more accessible and less technical side, so I have also made some decisions about content. There is something here from each of the areas in which Congar wrote — ecumenism, ecclesiology, history of theology, pneumatology, and the role of the laity in the Church — but for the most part I have chosen to highlight the last of these items, his pervasive interest in the place of the laity in the future of the Church, since this may be his most lasting influence and is certainly the dimension of his work of most immediate significance at the present time. Congar knew very well that a theology of the laity is an ecclesiology and, indeed, that a Spirit-ecclesiology had important ramifications for the way in which a hierarchical Church should function. I am not sure that Congar would have welcomed all the changes that may soon happen in the Church, and I know that in his time he was a little skeptical of some possibilities. But what is beyond dispute is that he was an open-minded man who loved the Church and who had about him none of that most corrosive of Church vices, ecclesiastical cant. In fact, his diaries testify to his horror of all hypocrisy and insincerity, not a little of which affected his own life negatively.

In order to make these selections more easily readable I have removed all footnotes from the original texts. The only references you will find will be to scriptural passages, noted within the body of the text and a few brief footnotes identifying one or other individual mentioned by the author. I have also eliminated more abstruse or technical discussions with this or that book or theologian of his times, something Congar often included in his texts but that, of their nature, were of immediate rather than continuing significance. I have silently translated the occasional Latin phrase. The page references for the selections are included at the end of each passage. Anyone who wishes to follow Congar further into the discussions represented here can do so by turning to the actual book from which the selections are drawn, though in most but not all cases these are now out of print and can be found primarily in theological libraries.

My thanks for support with this project are due to a number of people, first among them Robert Ellsberg of Orbis Books, who has shown encouragement and patience in equal proportions. I also owe the customary but genuine debt of gratitude to the wonderful community of scholars with whom I work at Fairfield University, principal among whom (as always) is my good friend and colleague of many years, John Thiel. I am grateful too to Christopher Ruddy for his generous permission to reprint his translation of a passage of Congar on the virtue of patience, which previously appeared in the pages of *Commonweal,* the most outstanding Catholic journal of opinion published in the United States today. Other translations from the French are my own. Additionally, much of the work of preparing this manuscript involved scanning out of print books into Word documents and then painstakingly checking them for computer-induced errors. Carolyn Arnold began this process on my behalf in 2007, then passed it on to Jocelyn Collen, and it finally fell into the hands of my research assistant during the summers of 2008 and 2009, Anne Krane. To all three of these indefatigable women goes my gratitude for, literally, making this book possible. Finally, I thank my spouse, Beth Palmer, for letting me get on with it while pursuing her own equally important professional responsibilities, and my son, Jonathan Palmer Lakeland, for willingly staying out of my way without even having to be asked.

Sources

DBC *Dialogue between Christians: Catholic Contributions to Ecumenism*. Translated by Philip Loretz, S.J. Newman Press: Westminster, Md., 1966. Originally published as *Chrétiens en dialogue: Contributions catholiques à l'oecuménisme*. Paris: Cerf, 1964.

DC *Divided Christendom: A Catholic Study of the Problem of Reunion*. Translated by M. A. Bousfield. London: Centenary Press, 1939. Originally published as *Chrétiens désunis: Principes d'un "oecumenisme" catholique*. Paris: Cerf, 1937.

FSL *Faith and Spiritual Life*. Translated by A. Manson and L. C. Sheppard. New York: Herder and Herder, 1968. Originally published as Part II of *Les voies du Dieu vivant: Théologie et vie spirituelle*. Paris: Cerf, 1962.

FYCT *Fifty Years of Catholic Theology: Conversations with Yves Congar*. Edited and introduced by Bernard Lauret. Translated by John Bowden. Philadelphia: Fortress, 1988. Originally published as *Entretiens d'automne*. Paris: Cerf, 1987.

HS *I Believe in the Holy Spirit*. Translated by David Smith. New York: Crossroad, 1997. Originally published as *Je crois en l'Esprit Saint*. Paris: Cerf, 1979–80.

LCW *Laity, Church and World: Three Addresses by Yves Congar*. Translated by Donald Attwater. Baltimore: Helicon, 1960. Originally published as *Si vous êtes mes temoins*. Paris: Cerf, 1959.

LPC *Lay People in the Church: A Study for a Theology of the Laity.* Translated by Donald Attwater. Revised edition with additions by the author. London: Geoffrey Chapman, 1965. Originally published as *Jalons pour une théologie du laïcat.* Paris: Cerf, 1953, rev. ed. 1964.

MC *The Mystery of the Church.* Baltimore: Helicon, 1960. Originally published as *Esquisses du Mystère de l'Eglise.* Paris: Cerf, 1941.

PL *Priest and Layman.* Translated by P. J. Hepburne-Scott. London: Darton, Longman & Todd, 1967. Originally published as *Sacerdoce et laïcat.* Paris: Cerf, 1962.

PPC *Power and Poverty in the Church.* Translated by Jennifer Nicholson. Baltimore: Helicon, 1964. Originally published as *Pour une église servante et pauvre.* Paris: Cerf, 1963.

RG *The Revelation of God.* Translated by A. Manson and L. C. Sheppard. New York: Herder and Herder, 1968. Originally published as Part I of *Les voies du Dieu vivant: Théologie et vie spirituelle.* Paris: Cerf, 1962.

UV *Une vie pour la verité: Jean Puyo interroge le Père Congar.* Les Interviews Le Centurion. Paris: Centurion, 1975.

VFR *Vraie et fausse réforme dans l'Eglise.* Paris: Cerf, 1950.

WW *The Wide World My Parish: Salvation and Its Problems.* Baltimore: Helicon, 1961. Originally published as *Vaste monde, ma paroisse.* Paris: Témoignage Chrétien, 1959.

Introduction

I would have preferred to say nothing at all about myself.
—Yves Congar

The year 1904 was auspicious for the Church. In that year four great theologians saw the light of day for the first time, Karl Rahner, Bernard Lonergan, John Courtney Murray, and Yves Congar, four men all of whom in their different ways devoted their lives to the theological revolution that would in the second half of the twentieth century sweep away the ultramontane, neoscholastic, and plainly world-hating mien of nineteenth-century Rome. With what is surely divine irony, it was just as Pius X was preparing his lamentable *Lamentabile* and the deplorable and destructive encyclical against the Modernist heresy, *Pascendi* (both 1907), that those who would undo much of the damage were born into the world.

Yves Congar made his entrance on April 13, in the north-east French town of Sedan, in the Ardennes, the youngest of four children.[1] While his early life with his two brothers and sister seems to have been happy and uneventful, things changed with the onset of World War I and the bombing and then the occupation of Sedan by the German armies. Sedan was a city of French patriots, none more so than the ten-year-old Congar, who began a diary he kept of the occupation in the following way:

> Here begins a tragic story, a sad and somber story written by a child who at heart has always had both respect for

1. There is no full-length biography of Yves Congar. The most extended biographical treatment available in English is the 1968 study by Congar's French Dominican brother, Jean-Pierre Joshua, *Yves Congar: Theology in Service of God's People* (Chicago: Priory Press). Next best is Elizabeth Groppe's short biography in Britannica Online (*www.britannica.com/EBchecked/topic/1337403/Yves-Congar*).

> his fatherland and a just and tremendous hatred for a cruel and unjust people.[2]

By the end of the war in 1918 the young Congar had decided he wanted to become a priest, undoubtedly in some part motivated by the harshness of life under the occupation and feeling that as a priest he might be able to help deal with life's more difficult side. In an autobiographical sketch he wrote in the late 1940s he dates his realization of a priestly vocation to the spring of 1918. Prior to that time, he says, he had thought he might become a medical doctor or enter the military either as a doctor or as a plain soldier. But that fateful spring he was filled with an almost palpable feeling of inner emptiness, until an inner voice questioned, "So should I become a priest? . . . Am I sent to France to bring it back to God. Should I preach to men to convert them?"[3]

So off he went in 1919 to the minor seminary and then on to Paris from 1921 to 1924, to the Institut Catholique, for the required philosophical studies for priesthood. At this time he knew nothing of Dominicans, but after a compulsory year of military service and a little further heart-searching, he entered the Dominican novitiate in Amiens in 1925, and then went on to theology studies at Le Saulchoir in Belgium, where the French Dominicans had established their seminary after having been expelled from France at the turn of the century. Congar was ordained on July 25, 1930, and two years later started to teach at Le Saulchoir. Thus began a life's work that ended only with his death in Paris on June 22, 1995. No Catholic theologian, not even those other distinguished individuals who shared his

---

2. Quoted in Jossua, *Yves Congar,* 12. The entire text is available in French as *Journal de la guerre, 1914–1918* (Paris: Cerf, 1997) and is quoted extensively in Svetlana Palmer and Sarah Wallis, *Intimate Voices from the First World War* (New York: William Morrow, 2004), esp. 43–68.

3. "Mon témoignage" in *Journal d'un théologien (1946–56),* edited by Etienne Fouilloux (Paris: Cerf, 2001), 19–62. This reference, p. 30.

birth-year, had a greater influence on the course of twentieth-century Catholic theology than the subject of this selection of writings.

Biographers often look for "early influences" to explain the later development of their subject's life. The child is father to the man, we are often told. Certainly for Congar the years of German occupation of Sedan seem to have been very influential. It was then that he seemed to develop the natural stoicism and self-discipline that those who knew him often commented upon later in life. But more significant might be the early stirrings of ecumenism, his first and perhaps last theological love. Congar tells us himself of spending time as a fourteen-year-old arguing with his Protestant friend about the sacrifice of the Mass, and he had many Protestant and Jewish friends in his early years in Sedan. But, he says, there was a "more mystical connection" to Protestantism:

> Our parish Church, which was situated in a suburb of our little town of Sedan, had been deliberately set on fire by the Uhlans when they entered Sedan on August 25, 1914. The [Lutheran] pastor, M. Cosson, offered our Curé a little Protestant chapel right next to my parents' garden and for the next six years this served as our parish Church.

Here, thought Congar, was where his vocation to ecumenism was somehow kindled, and he "was often fired with a desire to make some return to the Protestants" for their generosity.[4]

Congar's seminary formation also gave him a number of experiences that, when later sorted through, would explain his characteristic set of priorities and his prevailing no-nonsense attitude about his beloved Catholic tradition. While studying

---

4. Congar's words are taken from a lengthy autobiographical preface to a collection of his essays on ecumenical themes, *Dialogue between Christians: Catholic Contributions to Ecumenism* (Westminster, Md.: Newman, 1966), 4. The entire preface, entitled "The Call and the Quest, 1929–1963," occupies pp. 1–51 of that work. It overlaps considerably with the short memoir cited in n. 3 above, especially in the account of Congar's early years.

philosophy in Paris, for example, he came into contact with the lay Thomist philosopher Jacques Maritain (1882–1973) and with the distinguished theologian Father Reginald Garrigou-Lagrange (1877–1964). With the former he remained close for many years, while Garrigou-Lagrange eventually became a sworn enemy of Congar's theological outlook. Indeed it was the older Dominican who christened it, contemptuously, *la nouvelle théologie,* and who went on to aid Pius XII in the construction of his 1950 encyclical, *Humani generis,* which attempted to do for the "new theology" what Pius X had done for Modernism, in other words, destroy it. In theological studies at Le Saulchoir, on the other hand, Congar met important formative influences in the persons of Ambrose Gardeil (1859–1931), the prefect of studies, and especially in the young priest-professor Marie-Dominique Chenu (1895–1990), who like Congar was destined to play a major role at the Second Vatican Council. From these two he learned the importance of scriptural, patristic, and historical scholarship for the discipline of theology. All three elements became combined in the new theology in general and in Congar's work in particular to form what later came to be called *ressourcement,* or return to the sources, the other side of the *aggiornamento* ("updating") coin. These two impulses together marked Congar among other significant theologians with whom he worked, and through them the theological outlook of Vatican II.

The story of Congar's life from this point on is available to us in a number of places, though most of them are partial or even fragmentary. There are, of course, innumerable references to him and his work in books, letters, and diaries by those with whom he came into contact, though relatively little of the man himself becomes apparent in most of them. He is largely known through his work, which is certainly the way he would have wanted it. The exceptions lie in his own autobiographical writings, his enormously interesting diaries, two books of interviews with the elderly Congar, and a 1968 book by his friend and fellow Dominican Jean Pierre Jossua. Unfortunately, a number of these, the diaries in particular, are not available in English translation. While there are countless books devoted in whole or in part to his theology, there is no full-length biography. Consequently, coming to appreciate Congar the man is possible only by pulling a remark or two from here, an observation from there, and a quick sketch from somewhere else.

In his introduction to the 1966 volume *Dialogue between Christians,* which collected a number of important articles on various aspects of ecumenism, Congar explains at some length the challenges of his early years as an ecumenist. It was in 1929, he writes, when he had already determined on ecclesiology as his theological focus that, while meditating on chapter 17 of John's Gospel, he "recognized [his] vocation to work for the unity of all who believe in Jesus Christ."[5] From the time of his ordination he made clear his intention to work in the field of ecumenism and received no opposition from his Dominican superiors. In the early 1930s he made multiple contacts with leading Protestant scholars, and "made a fairly close study of Catholic modernism and Protestant liberalism, as fathered by Schleiermacher."[6] This early work culminated in the invitation to celebrate the Christian unity octave at the basilica of the Sacré Coeur in Montmartre, Paris, in January 1936. The eight lectures he gave there became the substance of his first book, *Chrétiens désunis* (1937, ET: *Divided Christendom,* 1939). While Congar later came to see this work as deficient, others continued to consider it as a landmark of Catholic ecumenism. It was undoubtedly an extraordinary accomplishment for a young man of thirty-three, though it led to all kinds of difficulties with the institutional authorities of the Roman Catholic Church, which in the end, brought Congar to choose the path of ecclesiology.

5. Ibid., 3.
6. Ibid., 11.

Congar's growing difficulty with the Church over his work for unity had, at its heart, an understanding of ecumenical theology that was threatening to a Church only just emerging from the Modernist crisis. Deeply influenced by his meetings with the abbé Couturier (1881–1946), the founder in 1935 of the octave of Christian unity, Congar saw his theological work complementing the spiritual efforts of the Abbé. Couturier, he writes, "transformed the octave of prayer, which was in danger of becoming the prayer of Catholics for the 'return' of *the others,* into a week of universal prayer for the unity of Christians." In Congar's view, unlikely to receive much sympathy from the Rome of that time, *all* are called to conversion, which begins in "a mood of repentance" and continues in begging for "the miracle of reunion which God alone can work in us by converting us all to himself."[7] Thus in the late 1930s he was simultaneously becoming the leading Catholic ecumenical theologian and a cause for concern at the Vatican. This came to a head when he was forbidden to attend the 1937 "Life and Work" conference in Oxford, England, in which he had planned to participate as an observer. The decision that he might not go was handed down by no less a person than Cardinal Eugenio Pacelli, secretary of state to Pope Pius XI and soon to replace him as pope.

The response to *Chrétiens désunis* was deeply distressing. While many theologians, Protestant and Catholic, hailed it as a groundbreaking work, Congar was called to Rome to meet the Dominican master general in 1939, to be told of "certain very serious difficulties" with his book. In 1941 he decided not to reprint the book, a decision he later regretted because the revised edition he intended never saw the light of day. He finished the revision in October 1948 and gave it to the master general, who sat on it for exactly two years and returned it with the advice that he should avoid "false irenism." The lenses in his theological

7. Ibid., 20.

spectacles were, it seems, way too rosy, though in fairness to the general it might well have been that he had advance knowledge of the imminent publication of *Humani generis,* Pius XII's critique of the "new theology," and wished to spare Congar further pain. Two anonymous reviewers had read the text. One had no problems with its publication, while the other — in a clearly Kafkaesque moment — called for changes, while the substance of his comments was never passed along to Congar.

While Congar continued throughout his life to identify ecumenism as one of his major concerns, after his return from incarceration in German prison camps during World War II, he began to make the sideways move into ecclesiology. Though for many years he continued to preach the Christian unity octave in major cities all over France, his academic research and writing turned to questions of tradition, reform, and the place of the laity in the Catholic Church. He saw no break with ecumenism in this shift to ecclesiology. He made the move, he says, because of his conviction "of the inseparable connection between the massive process of denudation which ecumenism demanded and the ecclesiological, pastoral, biblical and liturgical movements." He continued:

> It seemed to me that each individual's ecumenical task lay in the first place at home among his own people. Our business was to rotate the Catholic Church through a few degrees on its own axis in the direction of convergence toward others and a possible unanimity with them, in accordance with a deeper and closer fidelity to our unique source or our common sources.

So, thought Congar, his later great works on reform in the Church, on the role of the laity, and on tradition were "successive applications" of the ideas "sketched out" in *Chrétiens désunis.*[8] But it is nevertheless almost certainly true that were

8. Ibid., 21.

it not for Roman and some French opposition, he would have remained a force in ecumenical dialogue.

In the middle period of his working life, from 1945 until around 1970, he wrote most of the great theological works by which he is best known, books like *Jalons pour une théologie du laîcat* (1953; rev. ed. 1964; ET: *Lay People in the Church,* 1954/1965), *Tradition et les traditions* (1960, ET: *Tradition and Traditions,* 1966), and *Vraie et fausse réforme dans l'Eglise* (*True and False Reform in the Church,* 1950, never translated into English). These years also saw extraordinary shifts in Congar's fortunes. In 1945 he had just returned from three years in Nazi prison camps, during which he had heard of the condemnation of his mentor, Marie-Dominique Chenu, and his removal from the rectorship of Le Saulchoir. Chenu was accused, wholly unfairly, of Modernism, and Congar never came to terms with this outrageous act, though he was prevailed upon in 1945 to accept it and not fight it further. As he wrote at the time, in sadness, "I collaborated," though he refused to replace Chenu as rector. And he added: "I would wish, on my deathbed, getting ready to appear before God, to have the strength and lucidity to declare solemnly that Father Chenu had been condemned unjustly by a miserable group of mediocre, ignorant, and characterless people."[9]

In 1945 Congar found himself living in Paris at a time that he later famously described as "one of the finest moments in the life of the Church" in France.[10] This was the France of the Young Christian Workers, the France of the new Worker Priest movement, France out from under the heel of German occupation, France of extraordinary hopes. This was the time of the Mission de France and the Mission de Paris, initiatives to bring the Gospel to the un-evangelized urban masses. Led respectively by Cardinal Suhard[11] and Father Henri

9. *Journal d'un théologien,* 54.

10. *Dialogue,* 32.

11. Cardinal Emmanuel Suhard (1874–1949) was archbishop of Paris from 1940 until his death, having previously served as archbishop of Rheims.

Godin,[12] these movements, especially the latter, made great use of laypeople in the work of evangelization. Godin in particular was a deeply inductive thinker, always trying to start from experience rather than from ideas or theories, a direction that put the two movements in a somewhat different position than that of the ecclesiastically sanctioned Catholic Action, and that may have led in part to the official disapproval they came to share with the worker priests. Though Congar wrote of Catholic Action at length, his own instincts seemed to lie more with the experientially based approach of the Young Christian Workers.

These hopes, at least ecclesiastically, were dashed for Congar in the growing caution of Pius XII's papacy, which reached its culmination in 1950 with the ecumenical embarrassment caused by the dogmatic definition of the Assumption of the Blessed Virgin, a doctrine particularly difficult to find even hinted at in Scripture, and with the publication of *Humani generis.* Within a year or two he was in exile, at first under virtual house arrest in the Dominican friary in Cambridge, England, and later in Jerusalem.

But the wheel kept turning, and the death of Pius XII and the election of John XXIII began the personal rehabilitation that led to Congar being, by most estimates, the single most important theological influence on Vatican II. From then on, he never looked back, working with great energy despite enormous physical pain at times for a further quarter of a century, becoming, indeed, a theological icon.

Congar's fortunes changed with the accession of John XXIII (1958–63) to the papacy and the calling of the Second Vatican Council. As you read the earlier selections from Congar's writings in this present collection you will undoubtedly see the extent to which the Council, and through it the whole Church, is indebted to the work of this great man. Congar's stamp can

---

12. Henri Godin (1906–44) was a French priest and author who played a major role in advising the Young Christian Workers in France during the 1930s and through World War II.

be seen most clearly on the central document of the Council, the Dogmatic Constitution on the Church, *Lumen gentium,* especially the definition of laypeople as "secular" and the central role given to the image of the Church as "the people of God." Perhaps more significantly still, as you read on into later passages, you will see Congar's approach shifting somewhat, growing more sensitive, regretting his earlier failures to break out of standard, classical divisions of the Church (clergy/laity, for example) or of the theological enterprise itself. Nowhere is this clearer than in the introduction to his revised edition of *Lay People in the Church* (1964), where he criticizes himself for too narrowly understanding the role and nature of the laity as "secular" and introduces a series of emendations to the earlier work that prepare the way for an even greater shift in his thought, from clergy/laity to the notion of "different ministries."

During his years of trial in the 1940s and 1950s and throughout the Council, Congar meticulously kept a diary in which he recorded his observations and feelings about what was happening to the Church and, to some degree, to him.[13] A private man who promoted the virtues of patience and humility and who continued to work steadily through the long years of suspicion, he was nevertheless a person of strong feelings and, at times, acid wit and even some overly harsh judgments. These characteristics, products of understandable frustration with systems and figures in authority, occasionally flared up in public but were for the most part reserved to the pages of the diaries, mingled with profound observations and important judgments. Called to Rome in 1946 to try to settle the fortunes of the Dominican house of studies at Le Saulchoir after the removal of Marie-Dominique Chenu, Congar, as noted above, refused the position of rector. In his daily journal of that visit he describes the two intellectual challenges of the Church in his day as subjectivity and historicity, dealt with creatively by Newman[14] and

13. *Journal d'un théologien* and *Mon journal du concile* (2 vols.).

14. John Henry Newman (1801–90), one-time Anglican priest, later Catholic theologian and cardinal.

Möhler[15] and less successfully by the Modernists. Seeing historicity and subjectivity as two closely related themes, Congar writes that "our mission is to see that this double movement succeeds," and comments that it was this effort that led to the condemnation of Chenu "by less farsighted men, inflamed by ignorant disciples of Garrigou, or by the petty-minded, the spiteful, and the vindictively jealous."[16] This volume goes on to chart the course of growing suspicion and oppression through the publication of *Humani generis,* the threats to his book on "true and false reform in the Church," and the 1954 "crisis" as a result of which he was sent into exile (more like house arrest) in Cambridge, England.

There, in September of 1956, he wrote a remarkable letter to his mother on the occasion of her eightieth birthday in which he pours out the intensity of his feelings about the state of the Church and the way in which his life has been affected by ecclesiastical censure. "The present pope," he writes, "has since 1950 developed to the point of obsession a paternalistic regime in which he and he alone tells everyone and each individual what he must think and do. He wants to reduce theologians to commenting upon his statements and not at all to do their own thinking, to undertake anything other than this commentary. Except, I repeat, a narrow range of carefully prescribed problems of no consequence." "The French Dominicans," he continues, "have been persecuted and reduced to silence . . . because they were the only ones to have a measure of freedom of thought, action, and expression. . . . It is quite clear to me that Rome wants and has ever wanted only one thing: the affirmation of its own authority. Everything else is interesting only as matter over which to exercise this authority. Apart from a few cases of men of holiness and initiative, the entire history of Rome is the demand for its authority and the destruction of

15. Johann Adam Möhler (1796–1838), distinguished theologian of the Catholic "Tübingen School."

16. *Journal d'un théologien,* 70.

everything that cannot be reduced to submission."[17] Turning to his own situation, he is even more forthright:

> Practically speaking they have destroyed me. Insofar as they are capable, they have destroyed me. All that I have believed and worked for has been withdrawn: ecumenism (I have done little or nothing since 1939), teaching, advising, work with priests, involvement in *Témoignages,*[18] participation in big congresses. They have not touched my body; in principle, they have not touched my soul; they have asked nothing of me. But personhood is not limited to skin and soul. Above all if a man is a teacher, he *is* his action, he *is* his friendships, his acquaintances, he *is* his influence. They have taken all this away from me. They have reduced me to nothing and so they have destroyed me. When at times I look back at what I have wanted to be and do, what I have begun to do, I am heartbroken. And I know there is no cure. I know them. I know that when they are after someone, it is until death.... It is an atrocity, a living death.[19]

Congar wrote these words after almost three years of exile, with no end in sight, but in fact on the brink of great changes. He thought he might be in this position for twenty-five or thirty years, until the end of his life, yet barely two months later he was allowed to return to France, in fact to Strasbourg, where he lived for eleven years before finally going home to Le Saulchoir at the beginning of 1968. But the biggest surprise came in July of 1960 when Congar read in *La Croix* the news that he had been made a consulter to the preparatory theological commission for the upcoming Council that Pope John XXIII had called about a year and a half earlier.

It is also in the diaries that we see how extraordinarily hard he worked in the service of the Council. Moreover, they serve,

17. Ibid., 425–26.
18. *Témoignages Chretiéns,* a leading French journal of the period.
19. *Journal d'un théologien,* 427.

no less importantly, as one of the most detailed accounts of the day-to-day doings of the Council at work.

Congar lived a long life, and its last thirty years from the end of the Council showed no let-up in his intellectual activity, resulting in one further major work, the three-volume *Je crois en l'Esprit Saint* (1979–80, ET: *I Believe in the Holy Spirit,* 1983). He also published a number of collections of his essays and his output—though never anything but academic—became distinctly more pastoral in intent. He also suffered terribly from illnesses that made travel, in particular, exceptionally difficult for him. But he remained a theological workaholic to the end, illustrating very clearly his fidelity to his youthful recognition of the gifts that the Spirit had given him and his conviction that he had to make maximum possible use of them for the good of the Church. If he paid the price of a certain isolation, as Jean-Pierre Jossua has suggested, he paid it willingly. Whether he worked just a bit too hard, as Jossua also implies, and as we might say today "didn't have much of a life," is pure speculation, though it is hard to imagine him ever retiring. And he never did, working as best he could right up until the end.

One of the better resources for reviewing these later years is a pair of book-length interviews Congar gave during his later years, one in 1975[20] and one in 1987 toward the end of his life.[21] The first of these two has never been translated into English, a great pity for many reasons, not least the charming details Congar gives of his childhood. He recounts, for example, how he and his brothers made an imaginary world out of the field adjacent to his house on the edge of the city of Sedan. It was, he says, "our beautiful kingdom of freedom. Our parents left us entirely free. We divided up the land into four 'kingdoms' without any precise frontiers. The prairie was our Far West and

20. *Une vie pour la verité: Jean Puyo interroge le Père Congar* (Paris: Editions de Centurion, 1975).

21. *Fifty Years of Catholic Theology: Conversations with Yves Congar,* ed. Bernard Lauret, trans. John Bowden (Philadelphia: Fortress, 1988). Originally published as *Entretiens d'automne* (Paris: Cerf, 1987).

we were the Mohicans. In the woods we climbed the trees and we settled securely between two huge branches like we were in a bird's nest. Sometimes we slept in our nest.... The children of the local farmers were our playmates. We organized wars in which battles were conducted with rocks. We climbed up the hills. We took prisoners."[22] They were, in other words, ordinary children in a world about to be interrupted by the coming of the Great War, of which Congar told in the diary he kept of those days.

Among the many fascinating exchanges between Puyo and Congar, already in 1975 suffering from the long-term illness that sapped his energies and restricted his contact with the wider world,[23] is this one in which Congar explains his attachment to Thomas Aquinas. "Could you briefly sum up the thought of St. Thomas?" is the outrageous question from Puyo. Congar replies, doubtless hiding his impatience:

> I can, if you wish, try to explain what he has meant to me. As a Dominican, as a friar of the Order of Preachers, I worship Truth. The motto of our Order is "Truth." This is a bit abstract, you may think. Not so much! I recently came across this thought from Mme. Swetchine:[24] "I love truth like one loves a person." I agree. I do not ignore the fact that it can be dangerous. Pascal said that one can make Truth into an idol. This is true. But the search for Truth can inspire a whole life. This is what I believe I have seen in the work of St. Thomas. This is what explains my attachment to his thought.
>
> I also love his intellectual rigor. St. Thomas has enlightened my spirit. I think I can say this without misunderstanding my limitations. I love the way in which he tackles

22. Puyo interview, *Une vie pour la verité*, 9–10.

23. A form of sclerosis diagnosed as early as 1935 but becoming progressively more debilitating.

24. Sophie-Jeanne Soymonof Swetchine (1752–1857), Russian-born French literary figure of enormous influence, whose correspondence was published posthumously.

> questions. He always tries to find, in each case, the basic principle and the conclusion, the cause and the effect. Truth is thus constructed, as if it were a tree, with a trunk, large branches and small branches. Thomism — truly — is the victory of clarity.
>
> I have been aware of it throughout my life. At the time of my first ecumenical forays, during which, after an Orthodox and a Protestant, I had expounded Catholic thinking on the subject of the cross, a young student — a mathematician — said to me: "Father, you have reconciled me to St. Thomas." How can that be, I asked, since I didn't refer to him even once? And he answered, "It was the order in your presentation." I owe to St. Thomas the virtue of clarity that I have never stopped trying to achieve throughout my work.
>
> St. Thomas is my master for another reason. He taught me to study the *formal* aspect of a question. A lot of discussions go round and round in circles and end up in an impasse because the participants are not all talking about the same thing. One says, "Churchill is a great politician." The other answers, "He is a bad painter." To speak formally about a question is to speak from a particular point of view. You are right, says the disciple of St. Thomas, from this point of view, but from some other I cannot agree with you.
>
> In ecumenical dialogue I owe to this intellectual formation the capacity, for love of Truth, to uncover the positive aspects of the thought of this or that non-Catholic author, in what way the truth can be recognized, how perhaps it can be placed in a larger frame of reference.[25]

Puyo wasn't quite satisfied with this response and suggested that Thomas was far too theoretical or abstract in his approach, and so he wasn't much help in finding what is true. Congar wouldn't accept this judgment.

25. Puyo interview [UV] 38–40.

> This is true of the Thomism of certain Thomists (or pseudo-Thomists), but not that of St. Thomas himself.... St. Thomas died at the age of forty-nine (like St. Dominic). Well, he had spent his whole life looking for texts to prepare himself to enter in dialogue with the heretics of his own time. In the thirteenth century it was difficult to get authentic manuscripts of the Greek Fathers or of the Arab commentators on Aristotle. In the course of long trips that he took to Rome... he never stopped looking wherever he stayed for texts to bring his thought into confrontation with that of others. One cannot suspect him of having had dialogue only with himself! But his genius for abstraction was such that his followers, less talented than he, wanting to imitate him, could in fact become unglued from reality, despite the fact that his intellectual struggle was always at the service of reality.

Puyo suggested as a follow-up that there are too many Christian intellectuals who are out of touch with real people, only to find Congar humbly reflecting on how much that might be true of himself. Horrified, Puyo insisted that he didn't mean Congar, who replied:

> I willingly accept it. Because of my poor health I go out little and consequently I am deprived of some contact with everyday reality. People interest me, of course, I read, I receive visitors, but the danger exists....
>
> At Saulchoir we were somewhat preserved from this danger, thanks to people like Father Chenu, so talented at contact with people and so much more courageous than I. Thanks were also due to our contacts with the Young Christian Workers. These were decisive for me. I have always believed in theological and pastoral dialogue. I believe that what are most fruitful are not the answers but the questions. Answers that aren't answers to a question are just not answers. They are words that just churn on and on, like a car's engine with no clutch.

> I confess that my illness isolates me. I suffer from it, because I miss human contact. But I have tried, all my life, to be in dialogue with our brother Christians from other traditions, with laypeople, to be open on practical, pastoral matters.... I believe that I have received more than I have given. One is in dialogue when one is prepared to change something in one's own thinking because of what the other says. It is true that lots of our "dialogues" are only parallel monologues. True dialogue is a difficult art. I have sought to practice it, but I see very well how your criticism could apply. In particular, with reference to new problems raised by the younger generation. It takes me considerable effort to understand these questions. I only get there with great trouble, and then badly, inadequately. At least, I try to understand.[26]

Puyo also inquired insistently about the role Congar played at Vatican II. A good example is the following exchange about priesthood. He begins by asking what priesthood is in the Church, only to receive the response that Congar "avoids the word 'priesthood' as much as possible.... I am too afraid that the word raises up before the eyes of the uninformed solely the clerics, the parish priests, while the whole people of God is priestly." Puyo goes on to ask whether there is a radical difference between a baptized Christian and an ordained priest.

> Well, I would reply that yes, there is a very radical distinction, but perhaps not in the sense you imagine. A text of Pius XII asserts... that the priesthood of the baptized and of ordained ministers differ not only in degree but also in nature. For a long time I have struggled with the text, to the point that I tried in the theological commission to get the Council not to use it. They asked me to suggest alternatives; they were all judged to be inadequate, so they retained the formula of Pius XII, which you can find in

26. Puyo interview [UV] 38–42.

> paragraph 10 of *Lumen Gentium.* Today I accept the formula. Explained clearly, it does not fail to be of interest. What it wants to say is that the ordained priest is not a super-Christian, he does not have something "more," the priesthood of the Christian and of the priest do not differ in degree. That of the ordained priest is of a different kind, in the realm of ministry.[27]

Yves Congar ended his days a cardinal, though he was too ill to go to Rome to participate in the ceremony in which John Paul II conferred this honor upon him. There is surely an irony, perhaps something to learn in what we can surmise went through his head when he heard of his "elevation." In the 1940s Congar, Henri de Lubac, and Jean Daniélou were dubbed "the new theologians" by a man who saw them as theological bad boys. After 1950 they were subject to ecclesiastical censures and exiles of various kinds, forbidden either to publish or to teach. And after the Council, de Lubac, Daniélou, and, eventually, Congar all received the red hat. These theological pilgrimages of the twentieth century offer a lesson about history and tradition, about *aggiornamento* and *ressourcement,* all principal themes of *la nouvelle théologie* in general and the work of Congar in particular. And, of course, they may suggest to us that the suspect theologians of our present age, even those who come under ecclesiastical censure, may be the fêted cardinals of the future.

•

Sometimes I wonder, if Congar were alive today, where he would stand on the great issues that concern the Church. We can, obviously enough, never know the answer to such a question, but conjecture must surely be based on an estimation of his personality. Someone who never knew him speaks on such a topic only at his peril. Nevertheless, it is evident to me that while Congar was feisty and sometimes ill-tempered, he was

27. Puyo interview [UV] 200–201.

humble, flexible, and a man of prayer. He was erudite beyond belief, but profoundly interested in pastoral matters. He was impatient with the follies of the institution, but patient with the slow, even glacial, pace of change in theological understanding. He gave his life — almost to a fault — to the work of theology in the service of the Church, and he continued that work almost to the moment of his death, through a final twenty years or so of increasingly poor health and immobility. If I had to look for a twentieth-century theologian to canonize, I wouldn't look any further than this man, whose proudest accomplishment was that he was a poor Dominican friar, whose role model was Thomas Aquinas.

Congar grew up in a Church that divided its people into the clerics and the laity, but he reached the point of questioning the way that distinction worked to the detriment of the community of faith. From the experiences of his early life he acquired an ecumenical approach that was much too far ahead of a fearful Church and that he was never really able to develop in the way he would have liked. He saw the need for reform in the Church long before Vatican II, worked arduously through the years of preparation for the Council and the Council sessions themselves, and lived to express at least a little disappointment at the missed opportunities of the postconciliar years. All these examples and more of the way in which he transcended his own background suggest (to me at least) that while Congar might not merit the label "liberal," he would approach disputed questions fearlessly, concerned only for the right response rather than seeking to protect long-established positions or vested interests.

Running through all of Congar's work is the distinction between and relationship of two ecclesial principles, that of structure and that of life.[28] Fundamentally, for Congar, it is the hierarchical principle that gives the Church its structure, but it

28. I work this out in more detail in my book, *The Liberation of the Laity: In Search of an Accountable Church* (New York and London: Continuum, 2003), esp. 56–65.

is the community of faith that gives it life. One good example of how this works can be found in his discussion of the role of lay authority in the Church.[29] Lay authority has never been a matter of *ruling* the Church, thinks Congar (though you have to wonder about Constantine). It is "the business of the episcopate alone" to provide the structure of the Church. But arguing about this is not only fruitless, it is counter-productive, since it distracts attention from the real role of the laity, which, he writes, resides in "the principle of consent, a principle not of structure but of life, as a concrete law of all the great acts of ecclesial life, beginning with that of designation to the highest offices."[30] Lay cooperation brings life to the structure, and one of the principal ways in which this was worked out in the early Church was in lay involvement in the selection of bishops. The role of the laity was not determinative but it was a vital constituent of Church practice, at its healthiest in "the meeting and harmonizing between a hierarchical communication from above and a community's consent."[31]

With the distinction between structure and life firmly in mind, we can readily see the way in which Congar would move forward on contested issues in the Church today, or at least on some of them. Evidently, he would be inclined to support the overwhelming majority of today's American lay Catholics in their wish to have a greater say in the selection of their bishops and pastors. This is a "no brainer" for those who take seriously the role of lay consent in the life of the Church. He clearly thinks too that the laity need sometimes to speak out against clerical misbehavior, speaking favorably of lay zeal "when, in a sudden excess of enthusiasm they jump the barriers of protocol, and at their risk and peril cross the zone of silence and dignity behind which the priestly hierarchy too often isolates itself

29. *Lay People in the Church*, 234–70.
30. Ibid., 247.
31. Ibid., 263.

in order to protect the prestige of its authority and the stability of tradition."[32] At the very least, in the earlier part of his theological career, Congar was an example of the class of traditional clergy who maintain certain essentialist views about the prerogatives of ordination but who have the common sense and compassion to see the ills of clericalism. But what then are we to make of his later assertion that "now it is not the laity, but the clergy, that are in need of definition."

If the reader works through the texts collected here with an eye on when the various pieces were written, it will be readily apparent that as he grew older, Congar became more flexible and, frankly, more critical of day-to-day ecclesiastical goings-on. The critical moment for him probably came in the early 1950s with the destruction of the French Worker Priest movement, which he had so volubly supported, rapidly followed by his own exile and exclusion from professional life, which as we saw above had such a profoundly painful effect upon him. Political expediency was simply not part of his make-up. As we can see in his writings on St. Thomas included here and there in the present volume, commitment to truth was paramount for him, as a Dominican and as a Thomist theologian. It is not hard to imagine how terrible would be his judgment on the scandal of sexual abuse, and equally on the crime of cover-up or accommodation that so many bishops seem to have fallen into. It is also, I believe, not difficult to imagine him who pressed for the reintroduction of the permanent diaconate being ready and willing to consider the reintroduction of married clergy. His writings on the clergy evidence a conviction that mandatory celibacy in the Western Church was an important and necessary step at the time, because of historical and political circumstances, not because of some convincing theological argument. By the same token, if those circumstances have changed dramatically then the question, it would seem, could be reopened again. Priesthood, for Congar, is essentially about sacrifice, but

32. Ibid., 267.

then so is the life of the laity as illustrated in their role in the liturgical assembly. Congar would be unhappy with current efforts to remove the laity from significant liturgical roles, as he would celebrate the profusion of lay ministries apparent throughout the Church, nowhere more so than in North America. And while it would be difficult to make a case that Congar would favor liberation theology, it is certainly true that he promoted the importance of "small communities" and that he believed in the centrality of the (dare we say "preferential option" for the) poor and their concerns in the life of the Church, both of which are important pillars of liberationist ecclesiology.

Some of the flavor of Congar's flexibility and indeed delicacy of thought comes across in his comments to Bernard Lauret, late in life, on the phenomenon of liberation theology. Lauret asked Congar, in 1987, what he made of "theologies of liberation." Here is his answer, at some length, and it provides an appropriate way to end this present brief introduction to the work and thought of a great Christian theologian.

> I am acquainted with a certain number of well-known authors of this theology of liberation. I have close personal connections with Gustavo Gutiérrez,[33] and I know Leonardo Boff[34] extremely well. I know others like Pablo Richard,[35] but there are also those whom I do not know personally, like Jon Sobrino.[36] You will realize that their intention is to replace the theology of development on which Paul VI based his fine encyclical *Populorum progressio*.... But there is more here than development, because the very idea of liberation has come from the

33. Peruvian theologian and Dominican friar born in 1922. Generally considered the founder of liberation theology and author of the 1968 book *A Theology of Liberation.*

34. Brazilian liberation theologian born in 1938; former Franciscan priest.

35. Chilean priest and liberation theologian; born in 1939.

36. Jesuit priest and liberation theologian; born in Spain in 1938 but has worked most of his life in El Salvador.

awareness of a whole people that is both poor and Christian, that they must liberate themselves. That has been the starting point of this theology. What I have against some ideas, some accounts, and even the very first accounts by Ratzinger . . .[37] is that they connect liberation theology with European origins. Now it is true that Leonardo Boff studied in Germany, and indeed with Ratzinger, whose pupil he was, and that Gustavo Gutiérrez studied in Lyons. But that does not make liberation theology an application of European political theology, and if the liberation theologians have taken over certain concepts, even from Marxism — and have done so, moreover, in a way that can be and has been rightly criticized — that is not the real origin of their research. The true source of liberation theology is the specific experience of a poor Christian people that is aware of its situation and of its concern to free itself — on the basis of the gospel itself and in small basic communities. This is so basic that it produces a kind of epistemological structure that is not that of theological reflection of a Western kind, but is original. It is that which in my view has not been sufficiently recognized, even in Rome.[38]

---

37. Joseph Ratzinger, born in 1927, was professor at Regensburg in West Germany, later archbishop of Munich, and then prefect of the Congregation for the Doctrine of the Faith in the Vatican from 1989 until his elevation to the papacy as Benedict XVI in 2005.

38. Lauret, FYCT 83–84.

1

Congar the Ecumenist

Nothing is more like an evangelical who really prays than a Catholic who really prays. —Yves Congar

It was as an ecclesiologist that Congar first understood his theological vocation, but he soon turned to ecumenism. He burst upon the scene with the publication of Chrétiens désunis *(1937, ET:* Divided Christendom: A Catholic Study of the Problem of Reunion, *1939). There were many striking things about this book. By most estimates it was the first serious effort of a Catholic theologian to reflect upon the challenge of ecumenism, and it was far more warmly received by Protestant and Anglican scholars than by Catholic Church leaders. In his second book on ecumenical issues,* Dialogue between Christians: Catholic Contributions to Ecumenism *(1966), where he collected issues written over a twenty-year period, he reflected back on those early days in a lengthy introduction.*

I would have preferred to say nothing at all about myself. However, several friends asked me to record my own personal witness to ecumenism and to say what paths I followed, or better, what ways I actually passed through. I finally yielded to their friendly insistence when I was collecting a number of essays and articles, published in the last thirty years or so, and had reached the stage of assembling those dealing with ecumenism. The reader will not find here a complete account of my recollections. . . . Nor will there be any "confessions," though it would be a grateful task for me to praise God for the many mercies and the guidance that I have received, in a measure far beyond my merits. I simply wish to say how I came to ecumenism, how I endeavored to correspond to so clear a vocation, and how I was led to adopt a policy of discretion bordering upon reserve, if not of actual silence.

I do not normally keep a diary and have only done so in two sorts of circumstance: when I have been privileged to undergo a new experience in contact with a new world or when I have become involved in events of historic importance (war, the crisis of 1954, the Council). I have not been able to consult notes made from day to day nor to reread old letters, so my reconstruction of past events remains somewhat uncertain. Nevertheless, I am confident that I am not mistaken as regards the essentials.

I recognized my vocation to ecumenism in 1929, when I had already directed my studies to ecclesiology. (The subject I chose for my lectorate thesis in the summer of 1928 was "The Unity of the Church.") During three years in a Carmelite major seminary and four years of religious life as a Dominican, I offered myself daily to God, as best I could, for the accomplishment of his will. Every day, at Lauds, I recited the Benedictus, but one verse of the canticle was less said *by* me than said *within* me by another. *Et tu, puer, propheta altissimi vocaberis.* ("And you, child, will be called the prophet of the most high: for you will go before the Lord to prepare his ways.") I do not and did not ascribe this to any exceptional vocation or signal mission. What was said of John the Baptist is, in fact, said to every priest and, indeed, to every Christian. Each one of us is called upon to offer and to lay himself open daily for the faithful execution of his allotted part, however modest and obscure, in the realization at the appointed time of the design that the God of grace traces within the framework of human history. My ordination to the priesthood was approaching and I was due to receive it on July 25, 1930. As a preparation for it, I studied both the theology of the Eucharistic sacrifice, especially in Canon F. Masure's *The Christian Sacrifice* and the Gospel of St. John with the help of Père Lagrange[1] and of St. Thomas. It was while meditating upon the seventeenth chapter of St. John's Gospel that I clearly recognized my vocation to work for the unity of all who believe in Jesus Christ. Ever since the days immediately following my ordination, I have often repeated that prayer, especially when celebrating the votive Mass *pro unitate,* and while doing so the thought occurred to me that, as celebrant, the priest has a certain sacramental character and that in his prayer he also represents Christ.

I have said that it was then that I *realized* my ecumenical vocation, but the seeds of it had been sown in me for many years, no doubt even from my childhood. Very soon I discovered that a large number of circumstances and incidents had prepared me for it, some in an immediate and relatively specific manner, others more remotely — the first roots as it were. In the fervent atmosphere of Saulchoir, a strong liturgical interest did not prevent us from devoting very lively attention to other great causes in the Church insofar as we were acquainted with them....

In 1917–18, when I was thirteen or fourteen years old, my comrade was one of the sons of the pastor of our little town, and I conducted great theological discussions with him, chiefly about sacrifice and the Mass. In order to have something solid at my disposal, to which I could refer, I learned the Lauda Sion by heart, without, at the time, knowing anything about its author. When some question embarrassed me, I would try to find the basis for an answer in one of its strophes. Apart from all this, however, I had a more mystical contact with Protestantism. Our parish church, which was situated in a suburb of

---

1. Marie Joseph Lagrange (1885–1938), generally considered to be the founder of modern Catholic biblical scholarship.

our little town of Sedan, had been deliberately set on fire by the Uhlans when they entered Sedan on August 25, 1914. The pastor, M. Cosson, offered our curé a little Protestant chapel right next to my parents' garden and for the next six years this served as our parish church. It was in this chapel that my religious conscience was awakened during the hard and fervent years of the war and the occupation. If I neither received nor recognized my priestly vocation there, at least I was strengthened in it by my childish prayers in which I sought light and assurance from God. I have often thought about it since then and I cannot believe that my vocation to ecumenism has no connection with these circumstances. I was often fired with a desire to make some return to the Protestants for all I had received from them.

—DBC 5–6

The challenges Congar faced in fulfilling his vocation as an ecumenist stemmed from the hostility of the Church at the time to genuine work for Christian unity. What he wrote in 1939 would today seem tame to some, though to be honest there remain large sectors of Church leadership that would not give unqualified approval to the way he approached analyzing the problem of reunion.

In claiming for our Church that it is the true and only one, what do we make of other "Churches" and other baptized Christians, with their worship and their prayer? What is their Christian significance? And, moreover, is not a sincere Protestant, believing, truly consecrated to God and living a holy life, more really a member of the Church than a baptized Catholic who is slack and sinful or has perhaps lost his faith altogether? In one sense, obviously, the answer is Yes. But if that is so, what exactly is the point of this Church to which one can belong without being of it, and how are we to think of all this?

Only one answer seems logically possible. If we believe that the Catholic Church is the Church of Jesus Christ and veritably His Mystical Body, there is only one kind of recognition which we can, theologically speaking, accord to the Christian status of our separated brethren and the saved condition of the "good heathen," namely, the recognition that these are in fact our brethren and in some way members of the Catholic Church. That is a conclusion which we cannot evade.

But before approaching the problem that results from the fact that Christendom or the Mystical Body is not coterminous with the visible reality of the Church, we must try to throw light upon the fact itself.

The reason for it would seem to be that the Church is the Body of Christ *crucified.* The disproportion that we see is the extension and manifestation of a disproportion in the exercise by Christ Himself of the two prerogatives of His Priesthood and His Kingship. Christ the Savior is indeed Christ the King, but the Kingly prerogatives are, as it were, obscured, and to all appearance very nearly in abeyance for the benefit of His priestly work of salvation by the Cross. Though He had the right to the adoration of mankind and to the obedience even of natural forces, He came not to be ministered unto but to minister, in the form of a servant and not of a conqueror. He who could have asked of His Father twelve legions of angels bade Peter put back his sword into its sheath. Here on earth the Christ saves rather than reigns, and where he does reign it is not in a kingdom manifest in its perfection, but in an interior kingdom, hidden, crucified and crucifying — the economy of salvation by the Cross and not of triumphant kingship.

The disunion of Christians is verily a rending of Christ and a continuance of his passion. But it also testifies, with the multitude of the saved to some of whom He is not even a name, that He is a saving Victim, and that He came into the world to save it rather than to dominate it. This is the reason, as it seems to us, why His saving work reaches beyond the visible ark of salvation, the Catholic Church, and why the reality of His mercy as Savior surpasses the visible realm of His Kingship; why the Church, too, saves to a greater extent than she rules, and secretly incorporates more members than she can claim as subjects. From beginning to end the work of God in saving mankind follows the same law. Through all the course of history He has made Himself lowly, and if one can say so, strangely put Himself at our mercy. He will come again as Lord, for the perfect establishing of His kingdom, but now he comes above all as Savior, and knows for His own far more souls than the leaders of His Church can enumerate in their official returns. —DC 222–24

Congar's discussion of individual "dissident Christians," to use his somewhat unfortunate sounding term, is very generous. He is less open to the status of other Christian bodies and unmistakably argues that "reunion" needs to be understood as "return" to Catholic unity. However, he does not think that this will or should occur by the simple absorption of Protestant communities into the Catholic Church. In reunion, all are changed. Congar starts from the validly baptized non-Catholic child and argues that only God knows how many of these, as they become adults, "have not lost the grace and infused faith of their baptism," though he adds that "it is open to us to believe that the majority of dissidents are in completely good faith" (DC 234). He offers a striking comparison between the "good dissident" and the "bad Catholic," which may seem eerily familiar to those who know Vatican II's Lumen gentium, *where the bishops carefully spell out in section 8 of that document how everyone is somehow related to the people of God, their guiding image for the Church.*

The good dissident, so long as he remains dissident, will never enter, whatever he may do, into complete enjoyment of all the benefits entrusted to the people of the New Covenant for the realization of their communion with God. The bad Catholic, though he has lost grace and charity is, so long as he remains in the Church, in the Ark of salvation, and provided he does not deliberately leave it by a personal sin of schism or heresy, or is not cut off from it by a just excommunication, is in a milieu where the complete means of reconciliation and union with God are to be found. But he makes no use of them, while the good dissident does make use of what he has. The bad Catholic gives no glory to God: on the contrary, he offends Him, and is heading for final loss. The other does give glory to God, though imperfectly, and is on the way to be saved. The one has Catholic nationality, yet has not the Church for his fatherland. The other was born in a far country, and outwardly bears an alien nationality, but his true spiritual fatherland is the Church.

—DC 235

Congar next anticipates two objections to his position. First he faces the potential charge of trying to do away with the need for the Church by reducing it to "no more than the company of the just":

We do not say that the Church, in her unity, is *merely* the community of men whom God has justified because of their righteousness and obedience. What we do say is that the unity of the Church is an organic whole of all the principles by which God unites us to Himself as one people: that some of these principles may be found and be effective outside the visible institution which is the true Church, but also that the ultimate principles of unity, the seal of our communion with God, are found inalienably in the only Bride of Christ, and that even the most saintly dissidents are deprived of them. The principles are the fervor of sacramental charity, above all of the charity imparted by the Eucharist... and the right interior regulation of the adherence of faith and of Christian activity by the apostolic hierarchy. —DC 237

The second and contrary objection is that relative to the "dissidents" he may seem to be practicing a "kind of ecclesiastical imperialism of totalitarian appearance." While this reaction could follow from the use of the word "dissident" and Congar's commitment, carefully qualified, to the claim that "outside the Church there is no salvation," his defense is a strong one.

[T]he important thing to understand is the significance which all that we have said gives to the "return" or "conversion" of our separated brethren. We do not disguise the fact that we long for them to "return," nor do we disguise that in the last analysis . . . it is as a "return" that we must understand "reunion." Indeed, no Christian who believes in the unique truth of his own confession can understand it otherwise.

But this does not imply any clerical or even sectarian imperialism. What we seek is not the triumph of a particular form of institutional machinery as such, nor any particular system of doctrine as such, but precisely the triumph of supernatural life. The point is not that we call upon the dissident Christian to renounce one system in order to submit himself to another, but to fulfill within himself a life which has already been given to him and whose intrinsic dynamism is orientated toward this fulfillment. His baptism, just because it incorporates him into Christ, consecrates and empowers him for fullness of life in Christ, and, just because it makes him a member of the People of God, summons him to share to the full in the life of the Church. The seed of faith which is implanted in him in baptism aspires to its full growth in the acceptance and the public acknowledgment of the full content of the faith; therefore the acceptance of the full dogma of the Catholic Church will mean for him a leaving of the wilderness in order to enter into the full family life of his Father's house and the gaining of intimacy in the knowledge of the things of his Father. So also, the seed of charity implanted in his soul by baptism will find its full stature in reconciliation with his brethren and in the close communion of all creatures with their Creator. Again, to submit to the laws of the Catholic Church and to participate in her worship will be for him to find in his Father's house the fellowship of those whom baptism has made his brethren, to enter into intimacy with them and with the Father Himself. In no way does the "conversion" of our separated brethren involve an impoverishment or a repudiation of such riches as they already possess.

—DC 238–39

Congar's position on ecumenism in this early book is that ultimate success will depend on returning to the common sources of the Christian tradition and to "the interior life."

The source and the living principle of such an attitude as we have here outlined is an interior life which has grown beyond all partisan outlook and the clash of forms and systems and found the deep springs which nourish the life of the spirit. The man who lives on the surface, heeding the letter rather than the spirit, can find no mean between an indifferentism which will come to terms with anything and a rigidity which sets up one formula against another. A superficial life has no capacity to comprehend and unify, but the deeper the life the more it develops such powers of assimilation and response. Only the most profound life of all, that of our Lord himself, has the universal capacity to comprehend and satisfy. In Him and in the Church we find our contact with it. But the Church, so far as the exercise of it is concerned, very largely depends on us. It is in our power to make either a niggardly or a generous contribution to the extent and effectiveness of her ability to welcome and to satisfy.

Moreover, since action brings about reaction, in the end everyone gets the hearing he deserves. Whoever approaches souls in a rigid attitude of mind finds people with their backs up and a corresponding rigidity ready for defense against attack. But if we were to try to get back together to questions above all institutional paraphernalia to the common sources of life in all that truly lives, should we not find, far more often than we could have believed, that we had been meeting with a brother? It is not easy to express what we have in mind, for an unbalanced interpretation might make it seem either liberal or pragmatist, and it is far from being either the one or the other. It would be liberalism if we said that dogma, regarded as a relatively elaborated formulation of faith, is not true in itself and as such. It would be pragmatism if we belittled objective truth and supposed that nothing really mattered except the good life. But we say nothing of the kind. Only that behind the dogma as it is held institutionally by the mind the same dogma is linked with the living source, which is the grace of faith and the inner life of the Holy Spirit living in the Church. We do not say that dogma is an end in itself, though it has value in itself; its purpose is the life of faith animated by charity in the souls of men, for the Church is not an intellectual association but a fellowship in charity. The Holy Spirit who works in souls is One, as is the inward grace of faith and charity. The separated brethren in good faith are the temples of the Holy Spirit and their souls are interiorly stirred by a grace of membership and communion which tends of its nature to fulfillment in Catholic membership and communion. Experience here corresponds with theology and demonstrates that the profoundest needs of souls are everywhere the same, that nothing is more like an evangelical who really prays than a Catholic who really prays. Therefore, if, without indeed hiding anything or weakening our hold on dogma, we could contemplate it in its true relation to the living sources and in the spiritual perspective of the needs of souls and the work of the Holy Spirit, instead of disputing about it on the plane of complicated dialectic, might we not discover a spiritual fellowship which in itself could grow into communion in the fullness of truth? —DC 264–65

Congar's book Dialogue between Christians: Catholic Contributions to Ecumenism *is a collection of occasional pieces, prefaced by the lengthy autobiographical chapter from which we have quoted above. With hindsight into the later Congar's exploration of the theology of the Holy Spirit, the following brief chapter, originally written for* La Vie Intellectuelle *and published in 1950, is of great interest. It considers the call to ecumenism and the work of the Holy Spirit.*

There is no doubt that the cause of Christian unity exercises an attraction nowadays. And it is something more than an attraction, more than a mere sentiment or fashion. It is more like an uprising, a sort of great tidal wave sweeping into the hearts of men, amounting in many cases to a true vocation. In the twenty years or so during which I have been aware of my own vocation to it, especially when I have been preaching all over France (during the Christian unity octave, January 18–25), I have been privileged to see the growth and extension of this great flood and also to observe the erection against it of certain moles and dykes, the defenses of what has been aptly termed "embattled Christianity," especially the kind which has raised up bastions against the East, or against the Reform or even against the modern world as a whole.

This movement, which inspires men with the desire to serve the cause of Christian unity, is of a very pure and lofty spiritual nature. Like any other human endeavor, it may well have its flaws and weaknesses and may involve some danger of deviation. If, however, as is the case, it operates within the communion of the Church, these will be gradually rectified. A Catholic will take care to do nothing without the consent of his superiors, still less anything contrary to their wishes. From a practical point of view, this means that he will have to obtain the approbation of his bishop as soon as his activities become more or less public. If they become more public still, as for example through presence at one of the great ecumenical conferences, he will need the approval of the Holy See itself, which is the sign, center, and criterion of Catholic unity. Such was the precise meaning of the *monitum* issued by the Holy Office on the eve of the Amsterdam Assembly in June 1948. Cases may perhaps have arisen in which this or that individual failed to understand the urgent need for discipline of this kind, which is much more than an external regulation and expresses profound demands of Catholic communion and therefore, in the first place, of that very unity which we desire to promote. Such cases, however, must have been rare, and I personally have never directly encountered any. On the contrary, I have generally encountered an entirely genuine endeavor, yielding solid dividends of spiritual fervor, humility, and contrition together with complete loyalty to dogma and to the sacraments.

Initially, perhaps, it might have been feared that an interest in Protestant or Orthodox thought and life could lead to disaffection with regard to the teaching and life of the Church, for dogmatic indifferentism is often the forecourt of unbelief, or at least tepidity. Such considerations make the circumspection of the hierarchy understandable but fortunately the facts have provided decisive assurance on this score. The many priests, both here and abroad, who are engaged in ecumenical work and in contact with innumerable people sharing the same attraction unanimously testify that, far from leading to indifferentism, participation in the work for reconciliation and unity usually results in greater fervor, a deeper understanding of Christianity, and "peace and joy in the Holy Spirit" (Rom. 14:17). Personally I do not know of a single case in which prudently conducted ecumenical contacts have led to any sort of syncretism. On the contrary, I know of many who have been fortified by it and one priest assured me that he had witnessed the renewal of his whole parish through its conversion to the great cause of ecumenism. I myself would go even further and ascribe a very real, though unsought and unexpected, apologetic value to such efforts. Unbelievers are far more scandalized than we realize by the divisions among Christians. Although, unfortunately, we cannot yet show a united front, when we show that we are moving in that direction and that dissension and misunderstanding among Christians is at an end, then the world listens. People begin to feel that something new and important is happening in the way they expect from us. The lesson of experience drives home the strict truth of Christ's words: "That they may be one, so that the world may believe" (John 17:21).

The call to refashion the unity of Christendom is everywhere at work in countless souls. In a few weeks or months, at most, we shall once more enjoy the sight of nature beginning her life cycle afresh. How and by whom have all these seeds been put there; how do they continue to exploit the smallest plot of land in order to thrust down roots and send up shoots bearing foliage and fruit? The irresistible activity of the force we call life makes a magnificent spectacle as it spreads over the earth, fostered by the sun. The Holy Spirit is the sun of the soul and, at the same time, the wind "blowing where it will" (John 3:8), sowing the seed of its choice where no human hand has planted. He is also the life-thrust urging on its growth, and he provides the soil to nourish it. The work and the mark of the Holy Spirit can be recognized by the fact that men who do not know one another, or many various and apparently haphazard circumstances, should come together in the performance of some spiritual work in building up the Body of Christ. For it is in this way that he works. Men who gave no thought to it, together with uncoordinated happenings, are all made to serve the cause of unity, and that without any sort of violence or constraint; it is as though it were innate in them. The Holy Spirit dwells within men's hearts, at the very center of their being, and becomes himself their innermost inclination, their natural tendency. Himself immutable and unique, he is the living master of the impulse he imparts to each and makes all things converge upon that unity which is the proper outcome of his presence, for he is love.

That we are today enjoying a sort of ecumenical spring is manifest to anyone privileged to see the seeds of unity sending up shoots from ground where the wind of God alone has scattered it according to his hidden plan and purpose. The fruit which they will bring forth is God's secret and God's work. As unprofitable servants, it is our part to work and not to squander God' time, knowing that once the Lord's seed has fallen on the earth nothing can stop it from sending forth shoots, "as if a man should sleep and rise, night and day, and the seed should sprout and grow, he knows not how" (Mark 4:27). Thus, in a few years, in every country and in every Christian community, among laymen and among clerics, in the world and in the monasteries, among the learned and the simple, there is everywhere a blossoming and the hard, thorn-ridden earth grows green with new hope.

In 1925, a German Protestant theologian declared that the twentieth century would be the century of the Church. More exactly, would it be exaggeration to suggest that, by maintaining the magnificent foreign missionary effort of the nineteenth century and augmenting it with a missionary crusade at home, in Christian lands, our century may well go down in history as the threshold of an ecumenic age, a time when the Holy Spirit opened the eyes of Christendom to its scandalous dissensions and inspired it with desire for unity in a single Church?

Once again, the Holy Spirit accomplishes his mission of convincing us of sin, of recalling Jesus' words to us, and of leading us into all truth (John 16:8; 14:26; 16:13). The history of the Church shows that we come to understand the meaning of the Lord's words only little by little. It seems probable that we are still a long way from understanding even some quite simple things in the Gospel. Under the guidance of the Holy Spirit we are now perhaps being offered an opportunity to gain a better insight into the sinfulness and scandal of our divisions and to recall more vividly and effectually the Lord's words on unity, and thus enter afresh "into all truth." In conclusion, we could perhaps pause a moment to consider these three points.

The first step in the work of the Holy Spirit is to convince us of our sins, to awaken in us a realization that we are not all that we should be and, with God's grace, could be. This is fundamental for repentance, the taproot, as it were, from which the fruits of the Holy Spirit, enumerated by St. Paul, must spring (Gal. 5:22). No unitive endeavor can succeed unless it is based on a sense of our own guilt, of the ills we have inflicted on each other and an acknowledgment of it which really goes as far as the *mea culpa, mea maxima culpa* of which Karl Adam speaks. Möhler before him had written in his book *Symbolik:* "This is the point at which Catholics and Protestants will, in great multitudes, one day meet, and stretch a friendly hand one to the other. Both, conscious of guilt, must exclaim, 'We have all erred — it is the Church only which cannot err; we have all sinned — the Church only is spotless on earth.' " The contention that one particular party has invariably been right and that all the wrongs of history come from one side only might satisfy an apologetic whose purely verbal triumphs are illusory. The facts revealed by careful study do not support such a statement. We have a great deal to learn from an exact and objective historical investigation and we greatly need the inner unction of the Holy Spirit who instills in us the psychological manifestation of truth which is humility.

The Holy Spirit recalls Christ's words to us. He makes us mindful of them, not as one might by good fortune recall something for examination purposes, but rather in the biblical sense of remembering; he represents to us the living presence of the reality itself. In this particular instance, he arouses in us the memory of Christ's great prayer which occupies the seventeenth chapter of St. John's Gospel: "That they may be one." His manner of recalling it consists in making us penetrate the words more deeply, or rather he makes us more deeply penetrated by them; in short, he makes us pray them, for it is he who prays within us and makes us send up those sighs of which St. Paul speaks (Rom. 8:26–27). Because of this, the profound stirring behind our desire for unity is an impulse to pray as well as to repent. During the Christian unity octave in particular there is miraculous singlemindedness in divided Christendom in this respect. Our prayer must be deep rather than loud, expressing "the sighs too deep for words," which are not a mere display of emotion but issue from a profound need like hunger and thirst, the longing to love and to be loved, to share and to communicate with others, a fundamental and essential exigence, the desire to be a Christian. Let us not forget this in a few day's time when the unity octave will involve us all in a celebration which is so much more than a rite.

The Holy Spirit, then, leads us and guides us into "all truth." It seems to me that here we come to the point which corresponds most closely to the specific work of ecumenism which, by its very nature, is a movement toward accomplishment and plenitude. It envisages a unity of integration, not one of impoverishment; it seeks to reassemble and gather together. It demands from those of us who wish to serve it a great effort to broaden our minds and to develop our loyalty and fidelity in depth, the purpose being to surmount a complex of conventional ideas which, far from being in the true Catholic "tradition," represent its stagnation and attenuation. Yet, painful as such an effort is, it soon reaps its reward in the expansion of our own catholicity and in countless discoveries and enrichments. Beyond the purely confessional and somewhat narrow meaning of that fine name "catholic," we shall discover a truer sense of what we are and learn to become all that name implies, to make it a reality rather than a mere label and ourselves become more "catholic," more "universal." In doing this we shall rediscover parts of our heritage of which we never dreamed. We shall recover that part of our common heritage which our separated brethren retained in parting from us and which they have perceived, developed, and lived with greater intensity than we have. We shall not add truths, peculiar to them and lacking to us, to our own. We all believe in truth and we desire to be led "into all truth." For our separated brethren, this means substantial rediscoveries and, for ourselves, rediscovery, in greater depth and breadth, of our own tradition.

Clearly, it would be most undesirable and potentially very dangerous for any and every Christian to throw himself into the task of ecumenism with no other qualification than goodwill. There is scarcely any other field where improvisation and anarchy of this sort would produce more bitter fruit, and not every Christian is equally qualified to engage in ecumenical dialogue. We must also emphasize once more that any ecumenical activity which reaches a certain level of publicity must not only be submitted to a rigorous and indispensable internal discipline but must also conform to the external discipline of the Catholic community of which the hierarchy is the custodian. Nevertheless, when all this is said and done, the fact remains that the resumption of dialogue between separated Christians brings great enrichment to all. There is no doubt that the pressure and evidence of the facts has produced a general consensus on this point. When I wrote in this sense in 1937, it produced some astonishment, but since then I have received so much public testimony to it, sometimes reserved and sometimes striking, that it can now be regarded as common ground. As Catholics, however, we are not in quite the same position as our separated brethren. For them it is a question of the *esse* or substance of the apostolic faith; for us, it is a question of the *bene esse* or full development of tradition. It would be out of place for us to indulge in any false complacency on this account; on the contrary it should be a sober reminder of the grave responsibility which devolves upon us. Even if it were seriously maintained that the increasing insistence of successive popes on the duty of Catholics to study and understand their separated brethren represented nothing more than the prudent tactics of a belligerent in getting to know his enemy, it would still amount to an admission that there was something to be learned from the enemy. In fact this is not their motive. The popes urge us to make this effort primarily in order that we may learn to love our separated brethren and also because, in the words of Pius XI with reference to the Eastern Churches, "the fragments detached from gold-bearing rock themselves contain gold."

It is this gold which we wish to recover, to make a single offering of it all and to possess together in unity the fullness of God's work among men. —DBC 100–106

In 1984 Yves Congar's health made it imperative for him to leave the Dominican house in which he lived and the wonderful library of Le Saulchoir for permanent hospital care in Paris. There, over a period of two years, he responded to questions from Bernard Lauret, which were eventually published in a slim volume of Congar's mature thought on a whole variety of issues. Lauret pressed him in particular on the openness of Vatican II to world religions and on the relationship between the Church and salvation, prompting the following remarks.

It is a fact that missions have been in a state of crisis since Vatican II. But to tell the truth, they were already in crisis before the Council and it is for that quite specific reason that the commission on missions at the Council was so dominated by the missionary congregations. At that time, they were suffering from a lack of vocations and no longer had the verve they once had. So if there is a crisis, it goes back further. However, without doubt there has been a consistent crisis, sometimes a very severe one. Some people have gone so far as to say that we do not have to convert others; we simply have to help a Moslem to become a better Moslem, a Hindu, to become a better Hindu and so on. That is rather a defeatist reply....

I have my own personal position on this matter.... Instead of considering the question of religions as such... we should first look at the individuals who are themselves clearly bound up with a culture and a religion.... Now it is clear that for individuals, the culture in which they live and the religion associated with it are the ordinary ways of salvation, in the sense that "ordinary" usually has in almost all cases....

At all events, whatever position one holds it is inseparable from the dialogue which is characteristic of the Council and the Church which has emerged from the Council. The Church is the Church which held the Council and continues to live by it. A dialogue means that the others taking part in it are not just passive. At one time our view of these others could be summed up in the words of the psalm, "They were in the darkness of death": the missionary came, brought light, and all was well. That is too simplistic! Certainly the missionary does bring a light, but we have also to accept from the traditions of those to whom we come what can be integrated into our tradition — that, moreover, is what the Council texts say — and that takes a good deal of time, of patience....

Beyond question, we must still proclaim Jesus Christ.... To proclaim Jesus Christ it is not always necessary to speak of him or to preach him explicitly....

Speaking dogmatically, and that is more than theology, Jesus Christ is the absolute and unsurpassable religion in the sense that if there are intelligent beings on other planets than ours — and after all that is possible — while these beings would not have Jesus as savior, they would have him as Lord, as King, as the criterion of any possible relationship with God. From the moment when Jesus is God-man in a single person according to a unity of which there is no higher example, it is evident that he is the absolute religion, the fullness and the perfect example of the religious relationship. And he is that not by the exclusion of other factors, possibly other religions, but by inclusion. The perspective is changed a great deal when it is inclusive and not exclusive....

Clearly all that I have just said should be completed by a study on the meaning of salvation. People often talk about it: "religions of salvation," "Christ the Savior" and so on. But there are very few studies on the topic. The new theological development is only just beginning. The Catholic idea of salvation takes in all creation. Péguy said: "I would put into heaven whatever has succeeded."[2] I think that there is some truth to this comment and it makes a great impression on me that each year the liturgy makes Lent, the preparation for Easter, begin with the story of creation. And it takes it up again on Easter Eve. It is because there is a first creation that there is a second creation. It is because there is creation that there is redemption and that redemption takes in the whole of creation.

There is an extremely important insight here: in reality creation is already taken up into the paschal mystery toward which it ascends. So I too would put in my heaven whatever has succeeded. —FYCT 15–19

2. Charles Péguy (1873–1914), French poet and essayist; devout if nonpracticing Catholic.

2

Congar the Ecclesiologist

Just as Congar's early interest in ecclesiology had led him into ecumenism, so eventually he returned to ecclesiology. Ecumenism itself cannot be pursued without constant attention to the question about the nature of the Church. How can a Lutheran or an Orthodox Church leader engage the Catholic tradition without bringing ecclesiological issues into play? But it was probably the personal difficulties that Congar experienced over ecumenical issues, some of which we have noted above, that led him to refocus his energies on Catholic ecclesiology, though in the end he would find the challenges of being an ecclesiologist equally onerous. The bridge between his ecumenical and his more ecclesiological work can be illustrated in an essay he wrote originally in 1937, first published in German in 1941 and then included as the lead essay in the French book Esquisses du Mystère de l'Eglise *(Paris: Cerf, 1956). This in its turn became the first chapter in an English language collection,* The Mystery of the Church *(Baltimore: Helicon, 1960). In the final paragraphs of this essay, the English title of which is "The Church and Its Unity," Congar sees the outward form of the Church as subordinate to its fundamental reality in which it is coterminous with the life of grace of the whole human race.*

The Church shows itself, in the first place, as a group life which adapts itself, in some degree, to the progress of human society but which has its own rhythm, its particular existence, its laws, usages, rites, organization, activities, and hierarchy. Those who share in this life live in a parochial community where all its acts take place — birth followed by baptism, childhood with the first catechetical instruction and first Communion, Sunday Mass, various religious functions, feast days, special sermons, marriages, initiation of each new generation to prayer and the sacraments, funerals, anointing of the sick and viaticum.

In the parish there is a man who officiates at public prayer, administers the sacraments, teaches doctrine, gives advice, sees to the observance of Christian duties and "the laws of the Church." For whoever claims to be a believer is bound to certain practices and to the acceptance of a fairly considerable body of doctrines.

Above the parish, a priest of higher rank, invested with more extensive powers and in command of the others, is the upholder and expression of a larger unity, that of the diocese. But the religious community does not stop there, nor even at the whole aggregate of believers in the country. All Catholics throughout the world, regardless of differences in race, language, culture, and station, acknowledge themselves to be a single people, living the same life, sustained by the same hopes. One man, again, is the upholder of this unity and, at the same time, its symbol, one whom all call "the Holy Father." If such a multitude, differing in so many ways, lives truly in unity, it is because the Church has in him its visible head, its criterion of unity; he is obeyed as the visible Vicar of Jesus Christ.

Yet every bit of this — organization, laws and customs, rites and sacraments, works and joint efforts of every kind — has but one end: to further, beyond all human possibility of likelihood, a life of faith and love hidden in God with Christ. All this ceremonial observance, all this display, exists for no other cause than to arouse in the world faith and love for Christ and God. The claims made by the Church, its fierce insistence on its right to the education of children, its intransigence on doctrine and extreme reserve in regard to innovations, all has one aim: to unite souls to God by making them, through faith, the sacraments of faith, and love, living members of the Mystical Body of Christ. This Church, in fact, organized for action and powerfully constituted as a society, is, seen from within, a community living mystically with the dead, risen, and glorified Christ. The juridical implications of the ecclesiastical community have certainly developed in the Church but it is, nonetheless, no different in substance from the community in the cenacle which, intent on the preaching of the apostles, the common life, the breaking of bread and prayer, had but one heart and soul in Christ. Now as then there exists the assemblage of those called by God to be the beneficiaries of his inheritance, with the saints, in light. All its exterior life, all its social organization, are but an expression and an instrument of an interior life which is the life of Christ. The whole external and visible activity of the Church goes to enhance what is, indeed, its inner essence, the life of all mankind in Christ. —MC 51–52

The question of the place of the religious other relative to the Catholic Church is another ecclesiological issue with ecumenical implications. Congar addressed this problem directly in his 1959 book, The Wide World My Parish, *the whole of which is concerned with questions of salvation outside the Church. The following is the text of the brief chapter 3 from this book, entitled "Jacob's Ladder."*

We have seen that the Bible shows us God at work in the world according to a plan, raising up "first-fruits," that is, a part representing a whole and having a universal power. And it is from this background that we must approach the problems which we want to examine with the eye of faith: Christianity and other religions, the salvation of unbelievers, and of those who have never heard of Christ's Gospel. At the outset there are two ideas involved understanding of which is perhaps weak among us, but there are contemporary lines of thought that can help us to grasp them better: the ideas of *totality* and of *plan.*

There is a hallowed truth in personalism, the feeling for the unique value of every person; a person is a whole in himself, one cannot be substituted for another, he is the contrary of Koestler's definition of the individual in a communist society: "A mass of one million people divided by a million." But we must not lose sight of other truths. Every man and woman is a person, but they all have something else in common, their humanity. Mankind is made up of persons, but they are born one of another, they need one another in order to expand and develop, each one has his own destiny, but together they pursue a common cause: "The whole succession of men should be seen as one and the same man, continuing always to exist and to learn." The world too is a totality; science treats it more and more as a whole, made of the same stuff, and all held together by an aggregate of interactions, attractions, and compenetrations.

The world as a whole has movement and therefore a meaning. Materialism treats this movement and meaning as purely a result of forces within nature, though adding that it is man's business to interpret them by his intelligence and to apply his energies to them. But from the Christian point of view the world as a whole has a meaning which comes to it from God's plan. Plan and meaning are not simply those which the mind can recognize by carefully looking at things. Into the world taken as a whole, into the pattern of human history, God put the revelation and then the gift of something new; it was not contained within the energies of the world but, once given, it became its central point and constituted its meaning: the Covenant, fully actualized in Jesus Christ, who is indeed the union of God and man. Jesus is for the world, and the world is for Jesus: totality in quest of a meaning, and fullness of meaning. We cannot be sure that in Jesus Christ the world recognizes its meaning, but it is certain that he is that meaning.

Let me make a comparison. At one time I was living my life from day to day, and pretty happily, for my job was interesting. But, without having the sophisticated absurdity of Sartre's "Everything that exists is born for no purpose, continues through weakness, dies by chance," that life of mine was not illumined by the shining light of some clear purpose. Then one day I met somebody who put an idea into my head, something worthwhile, an undertaking, in which I recognized *the* meaning of my life; it not only determined my present and future, but threw light on the past, for everything had been pointing in this direction, although I had not realized it. Taken up with living and doing my work, I had overlooked it, but even so it was the meaning of my life; it made sense of everything and held the whole together. Boris Pasternak is right: "You have said that facts don't mean anything by themselves — not until a meaning is put into them. Well — the meaning you have to put into the facts to make them relevant to human beings is just that: it's Christianity, it's the mystery of personality."

If then, this is the place of Jesus Christ, we have to determine what is the consequent place of the Church, in relation to him and in relation to the world.

The Church is Church only because of Christ, but she is made up of human beings. She is a gathering of men among other gatherings of men, but bearing among them the mystery of Jesus Christ. She is the company of witnesses to him. *Inasmuch as it depends on men's faithfulness,* she brings Christ to the world, offering it opportunities to recognize him as the key to its destiny.

Provided we are careful not to turn a convenient and, surely, necessary distinction into a separation, it will be useful to look at the Church from each of two points of view: (1) as God's people, the community of Christians, she represents mankind toward Christ; (2) as institution, or sacrament of salvation, she represents Christ toward the world. Jacob "dreamed that he saw a ladder standing on the earth, with its top reaching up into heaven; a stairway for the angels of God to go up and come down" (Gen. 27:12; cf. John 1:51). Two mediations are joined in the Church, one going up, or representative, the other coming down, or sacramental; and through them she is the place where Christ gives himself to the world, and the world gives itself to Christ, the place where the two meet. In this twofold movement the Church actualizes the biblical idea of first-fruits. Coming from Christ and composed of men, she constantly bears the whole of one toward the whole of the other. When she takes root in some human grouping, there she makes Jesus Christ present and at work, that Son of God of whom St. Paul writes that it is God's pleasure "through him to win back *all things*, whether on earth or in heaven, into union with himself, making peace with them through his blood, shed on the cross" (Col. 1:20). No doubt this does not mean that all men, in the sense of each and every individual, will in fact be saved; it means that the act by which Christ makes the union effective is of itself really directed toward and includes all men, the totality of the world as such, offering all that is necessary for the achievement of the end that God has in view for them.

Since the Church makes Jesus Christ present and active to the world, all worth is finally judged by her, and it is in regard to her that men are seen to be blessed or rejected. Clement of Alexandria had this in mind when he wrote, early in the third century, "Just as God's will is a deed and it is called 'the world,' so his intention is man's salvation, and this is called 'the Church.' " That is not plainly seen as physical things are: "What do we see now? Not all things subject to him as yet" (Heb. 2:8). What St. Paul says of the Christian is not true of his personal life alone, but also of apostleship and of all that the Church does: "Your life is hidden away now with Christ in God. Christ is your life, and when he is made manifest, you too will be made manifest in glory with him" (Col. 3:3–4). It is true that to the eye of faith the Church never looks small in this great world. There she wears the best aspect she can, for the people she is able to reach. But, however modestly, she has always to seek to have and to show an appearance that *betokens* the Gospel, that *betokens* the Covenant, and a covenant that is in principle universal, for of that she is the sign and sacrament.

Each one of us for his own little world, all of us for the world at large — we are Jacob's ladder. The representative going up of mankind to God and the representative coming down of Jesus Christ to the world pass through us. The whole Church is sacramental and missionary, and so is each Christian in his degree. Each of the members of any group (e.g., a parish) that seeks Christ through the Church stands for the whole group. To what extent do they effectively aid the group in its journey to God? It cannot be known. But they are its first-fruits, a sheaf offered up, and they are intercessors for it: had there been ten righteous men in the city, God would have spared it (Gen. 18:3). We can only look ahead, and so we cannot see anything, for there is nothing to see in the future, unless with the eyes of faith and hope. It has been rightly observed that mankind goes forward in its history backward, because it only sees the road it has already traveled. When we reach the end, we shall see how the final result took shape in the beginnings, the first-fruits. And we shall give thanks.

The Church's twofold office of mediation entails a condition of power and of mission that is coextensive with her very existence. The Church exists in herself, as a sacred thing in the midst of the world, but she does not exist *for* herself: she has a mission to and a responsibility for the world. So at the Church's heart there is a sort of polarity, a tension or dialectic, which it is very important to understand. From the beginning Christians have been pulled in two directions, like someone hearing two calls at once. More exactly, they are thus pulled when they live their religion faithfully in its fullness, for if one call ousts or drowns the other the question arises how and on what terms unity can be had.

The first voice is that of another world. "Be not conformed to this world," urged St. Paul (Rom. 12:2). Were the Church to listen *only* to this call, she would become an association of the immaculate, a hand-picked group that would leave the world to its fate. She would be composed of people of the strictest practice, scrupulous in prayer and observances, sedulously cut off from the world, undisturbed by what happened to others. The second voice is that of this world and its enthralling destiny, the call of other men and the salvation of other men. Were they to follow *only* this call, Christians would simply become ardent champions of Progress, of History, of all those things whose names are written with capital letters, which for many people are in effect the only gods they explicitly acknowledge. It would then look as if Christianity were *nothing else than* the inner meaning of the world and a means to the happiness of human beings (that has happened in certain schools of thought, such as the Christian Socialism of Frederick Denison Maurice in England).

Now Christianity is that, but *because* it is *something else* first. It has a mission to the world and embraces it; but in the first place it exists in itself, as an institution coming from Jesus Christ, a people which testifies to him. Grain is for seed-time and harvest, but it has to be brought together, and it lives its own specific life.

According to the circumstances of the moment in the Church's history, Christians are more conscious now of one, now of her other aspect, the requirements of holiness or the calls of all-embracingness. The first Christian generations felt above all that they were the chosen ones, set apart from the world by knowledge and worship of the one true God. It would be very interesting to study from this point of view those early prayer texts that have come down to us, especially the eucharistic ones: that of the *Didache,* which goes back to the era of the Apostles, that of Clement of Rome, who was an immediate disciple of the Apostles, that of Hippolytus, of the early third century. But when we get to Sarapion's great eucharistic prayer (Egypt, early fourth century) we find Christians first giving thanks for the gift of knowledge of God and for the salvation he had wrought for them, and then praying thus:

> Lover of man, lover of the poor, reconciler of all, whom you draw to yourself through the coming of your well-beloved Son, . . . make us men who have life. . . . Give us a holy spirit that we may be able to speak and tell your unutterable mysteries. Let Wisdom speak in us, and the Holy Spirit too. . . .

The Church's universal concern finds voice there, as it does in the great intercession on Good Friday, in the litany of the saints, and, so profoundly and significantly, in the doxology that concludes the canon of the Mass: "Through him and with him and in him are given to you, God the almighty Father, in the unity of the Holy Spirit, all honor and all glory. . . . " It is clear that at that moment we can and ought to make our double mediation supremely real, becoming a Jacob's ladder with Jesus himself (John 1:51) and in the Church.

At bottom, the Church and the world need one another. The Church means salvation for the world, but the world means health for the Church: without the world there would be danger of her becoming wrapped up in her own sacredness and uniqueness. The idea of Church and world, not only as distinct, but as existing side by side, each "on its own," is not without value, especially from a juridical or political, and therefore diplomatic, point of view. But it is insufficient from a spiritual point of view, from that of full Christian existence; here Church and world are not side by side as in history, but closely entwined. They are not like two crowned sovereigns looking sideways at one another as they sit enthroned on the same dais; they are much more like the Good Samaritan holding in his arms the half-dead man, whom he will not leave because he has been sent to help him; or like a swimmer trying to drag a drowning but struggling man to shore. Georges Bernanos grasped this excellently:

> The Church is something alive, a force at work; but many pious people seem to believe, or pretend to believe, that she is simply a shelter, a place of refuge, a sort of spiritual

> hotel by the roadside from which they can have the pleasure of watching the passers-by, the chaps outside who are not hotel residents, walking about in the mud.[1]

Anxiety about "the others," that prompts us to bring faith to bear on certain questions, made Simone Weil frightened of shutting herself up in a society of the redeemed, of baptized persons who would refer to themselves as "us Christians."[2] She wrote that "the Devil says 'us' and makes other people say it." She did not see that, if "the others" are to be rescued, if the world is to be brought to Christ, we *must* first exist as "us Christians." Would to God we lived more that way, that we were more apart from the world and more clearly distinguishable from it, as the Israelites were distinguishable from the Egyptians by the lamb's blood on the lintels of their doors when God passed over! Would to God that we were more sensitive to the meaningful tension between the world and us! When he answered Simone Weil, Father J. M. Perrin brought the two requirements of goodness and completeness, of holiness and all-embracingness, into one:

> To come into the Church is not to cut oneself off from "the others." To have a home of one's own can lead to selfish exclusiveness; but it also can enable us to welcome and offer a home to others, helping them to draw nearer to God "in the house of the Father here below." If I may put it so, the others are separated from Christ only by a door that is always open.

A small Church in a large world; then, Christianity and other religions; and then, the salvation of "the others. . . ." At the level of social science there is no solution to the problem. But

---

1. Georges Bernanos (1888–1948), a Catholic novelist, was the author of *The Diary of a Country Priest* and other books.

2. Simone Weil (1909–43) was a French philosopher who was powerfully attracted to Catholicism but who ultimately felt that her vocation was to remain at the threshold of the Church without entering. She exchanged a series of letters with the Dominican priest Father J. M. Perrin about her views regarding baptism.

it is not set at that level; it is set by faith and by two truths of faith, Christ's divinity and the divine founding of the Church. A solution can be looked for only in what faith tells us: that this relatively little thing mediates between two great wholes, Jesus Christ and the world; that they are one for the other, and that the Church's mission is to bring them together and this in two directions, up and down, by representativeness and by sacrament, as has been explained.

Finally, we will make use of an effective comparison that we owe to our Protestant brothers, that of "The Church, the *Maquis* of the world."[3]

A king has been forced to seek refuge in a free country; his kingdom is occupied by invaders. From this far land he prepares a counter-invasion in force that shall achieve complete liberation. Meanwhile, in the occupied country, many people have come to terms with the invaders and even work in with them. Most of the people live from day to day, as best they can, waiting for deliverance; they are content occasionally to snatch a few minutes of the secret radio, much as lukewarm Catholics take a breather of Mass and sermon at Christmas and Easter, and that is all. But a certain number of men and women actively reject the enemy's yoke. (In our parable here "the enemy" of course means the Prince of this world and those malign powers that St. Paul speaks of — the worldly forces, both collective and personal, which seek to rule themselves, ignoring and even opposing the lordship of Christ.) These resisters, amid great hardships, strive to live as subjects of the free motherland they hope for and of their true king. They are tireless in their efforts toward liberation; and they are successful in enlisting the help of quite a lot of the half-indifferent, who give support to the resisters from time to time. But the resisters are disinterested men; they work for the liberation and happiness of everyone, without distinction.

3. The references to the "Maquis" are to the resistance movements in Nazi-occupied France. [Editor's note]

When the counter-invasion comes about, deliverance will be due to the resisters *as well as* to the regular military operations. Those people who have had no contacts with them or have despised and opposed them will then see in the resisters the first-fruits of their recovered freedom: a group representing themselves, who through every trial have kept alive the possibility of a happy future for *all.* This "all," however, will not mean every single individual, for a number of proved "collaborators" and traitors will be punished, but "all" in the sense of the general whole as such.

During those dark days of 1940–45 it used to be said, "A little Maquis in this big France — what do they think they can do against an enormous giant?" Very much as it is said, "A small Church in a large world. . . . " —WW 17–26

A few years later in Sacerdoce et laîcat *(ET:* Priest and Layman, *1967) Congar devoted a large number of pages to exploring the relationship between priests and laypeople, often very critical of his fellow clergy. Here is a brief passage from the end of chapter 14 of that book, which explores the background understanding of the Church that supports his conclusions.*

In conclusion I should like to define briefly the foundation of ecclesiological truth which is the source, when it is ignored, of the abuses revealed by history and, when it is honored, of the fruits and advantages revealed by experience and analysis. This foundation may be summed up in the three following points:

First, in giving the word "Church" its proper meaning. Having devoted myself since 1929 to the study of ecclesiology, I have made it my practice always to substitute mentally for the word "Church" its real meaning in the context, and similarly in the texts I read. The experience is perhaps disappointing, but instructive. In the majority of cases, and especially in modern official documents, the real meaning of the word is the hierarchy, the government of the Church, the pope and the Roman curia. On the contrary, in the writings of the Fathers and the liturgy, it is hardly ever wrong to substitute for *ecclesia* "the Christian community." The Fathers and the liturgy are also full of the idea, outlined above, of the spiritual motherhood which pertains to all the faithful with their priest. The work of the ministry is carried out by all the "saints"; the priests have to "organize" it. Their character as "mediators," on which much emphasis is laid, is very real. It is not exhausted by the hierarchical sense of the expression. Far from it: it comprises also, and decisively on the level of pastoral reality, the function of being the center in which the unity of the faithful is bound together, in the parish or the diocese. St. Basil writing a letter of consolation to the Church of Ancyra on the loss of its bishop compares him to the soul which binds together all the members of the body in one single communion. This first point is summed up in a few words, but its consequences are infinite.

In the second place, all that pertains to the juridical structure of the Church really belongs, and should be seen as belonging, to the heart of the reality of the Christian life, or of Christianity. This is the case, in particular, with the relation of superiority or subordination implied in the fact of authority. We must not posit authority first and in itself, and then say that it is wielded over Christians for spiritual ends, and must be used impartially, in a spirit of service. Christianity must be posited first, and then the fact of authority in it. In this way, it is qualified as Christian from its very roots; it is service, because the Christian life is service. We must first lay down the "with you I am a Christian," and then, included in it, "for you I am a bishop." To do this is to establish, from the outset, healthy relations between persons in authority and those who are subordinate. As for concrete expressions or interpretations of this healthiness, they can easily be imagined. Nowadays, thank God, we no longer lack good books expounding the subject, though they are not numerous.

Third, and last: the most comprehensive law of a healthy Christianity is that the Church should be the Church, that the world should be the world, and that both should be recognized for what they are, alike in their distinction, their opposition, and their necessary connection. It has sometimes happened that the world has been to some extent the Church, in the symbiosis of Christendom, when *ecclesia* denoted the Christian society. In those conditions, however, not only did the Church tend to adopt the ways of the world, but the tensions were readily transferred from without to within and were set up between the clergy and laity, or between distinct categories of clergy. When there is not really a world, there is not really a laity. If the world is not taken seriously, neither is the laity. When the Church is confronted with a world which is really a world, she is aware of herself, both as being *something else,* eschatological, and as having a mission to the world, and the responsibility for the world, for the sake of Jesus Christ and his kingdom. She is aware of being so in her entirety as community of the people called to the kingdom. She is structured, of course, but first she is living. In the Fathers, and for the liturgy, the Church is first of all baptism, by which a man exists in his state as Christian, member of the holy people, that is, *ipso facto,* in the state of witness for the world. At the day and hour when anyone comes to the faith, it is also required of him that he set his hand to the work of the vine, that is, the Catholic tradition. It is also an ecumenical truth. So I may be permitted to close . . . with a quotation from one of the founders of the Church of South India: "To be a layman in the Church means to be part of the mission of God in the world." —PL 259–61

*Reform, in fact, and the role of the laity in reform, had been the topic of a work that occupied him in the later part of the 1940s. "True and False Reform in the Church" (*Vraie et fausse reforme dans l'Église, *Paris: Cerf, 1950) was a text that played a large role in his being "exiled" for a time during the later years of the reign of Pius XII. It is also significant for its being the only major work of Congar never translated into English. In its early pages Congar writes of the Church as always in process of reform and specifically justifies the climate of self-criticism alive in France in 1946.*

In 1946 both laity and clergy raised their voices. They spoke neither the same language nor in the same tone, but there was a deep and impressive level of agreement between their protests and their desires. Those of the laity had the flavor of complaint; they bore the mark of the preaching they had heard, the liturgy at which they had assisted, the situation of working people in the Church, the old-fashioned, maladapted, unhelpful, purely bourgeois character of a great deal of parish ministry.... Clergy never would speak like laypeople. This is always the way. Not that clerics are bound to speak only in language that is sanctimonious [*bénissante*], hollow, or out of date, which is not the language of any true thinking human being, but because conscience and the exercise of priestly responsibilities impose moderation, reserve, concern to injure nothing and to take everything into account, everything the laity do not have to deal with. It is impossible for a pastor to be as radical as a layperson in his choices and his criticisms. —VFR 24–25

The critique of the Church on the part of today's Christians, that which we have gathered from some writings, has to be classified under the heading, "good critique." Not that everything is perfect. A fleshly man exists in each of us alongside the spiritual man, and their voices are often mixed together or alternate. Sometimes the one clearly gets the better of the other.

—VFR 38–39

He goes on to list the general characteristics of healthy contemporary self-criticism:

1. This Catholic self-criticism is frank, sometimes brutal. It absolutely does not follow from a lack of confidence in or love of the Church. On the contrary, it follows from a deep attachment and committed confidence despite certain real feelings of disappointment, because these are the disappointments of someone who loves and who expects a great deal, indeed, *from the Church*....

2. A second trait of today's self-criticism is its sense of responsibility. Not only, as we shall soon see, does it have its source in a real consciousness of the apostolic situation, but it has its history, one might say its intellectual preparation, of unarguable courage. Today's wave of reform could not happen without clear apostolic consciousness, any more than it could have happened without a theological and liturgical renewal of which the first artisans were Pope Leo XIII and Pope Pius X. It could not have happened without a renewed sense of the Church itself, clear above all in the last quarter century. The liturgical movement, with its reforming character, would not have been what it is if it had not been preceded and then sustained by the scientific work of researchers. It still finds support there. At the same time today's movement, which is essentially apostolic or pastoral, has a lot to do with the renewal of ideas about the Church, and it constantly refers to ecclesiology, of which pastoral work is only the prolongation or the application.

3. A third characteristic is the fact that, in the area about which we are speaking, the laity's role is substantial. A good number of more notable writings come from laypeople. This signifies a new consciousness on the part of the laity that they belong to the Church and that, in a certain sense, *they are the Church*. They consider the ecclesial issues that seem to them to be important. Who would not see in this new development the fruit of Catholic Action and of the challenge addressed to the laity by the Holy Father, to play their part in the burden of apostolic activity in the world, under the direction of the hierarchy?

4. Among the factors that make the present-day self-criticism serious and profound we have to cite the practice of returning to the sources, what is today called *ressourcement*. "Days are coming," says the Lord, "when I will send famine upon the land: not a famine of bread, or a thirst for water, but for hearing the word of the Lord" (Amos 8:11, NAB).

> The prophet speaks of a punishment, a withdrawal of the word of God. Today we live this text as a kind of blessing, since God has sent us, with the hunger to understand his word, an abundance of nourishment. —VFR 39–43

But Congar also thought that the reformer needed patience, surely a lesson that he learned the hard way. As a good and immensely learned historian, Congar always tried to take the long view, and here he writes eloquently about the need to distinguish between innovation and reform.[4]

The innovator, whose reform turns into schism, lacks patience. He does not respect the delays of God and of the Church, the delays of life. He moves with a rigid and exasperated logic toward "all-or-nothing" solutions, in which viable elements are cast off with all others. He all but puts the Church in the position of living to meet his demands, or else he quits it.

In order that reform be realized in the Church, it is necessary that it be accompanied by patience: by which I mean much more than watching the clock or presuming that everything takes time. I mean a certain disposition of soul and of spirit mindful of necessary delays, a certain humility and pliancy of spirit, the awareness of imperfections, even of inevitable ones. Jean Guitton believed it possible to characterize the Catholic mentality as one of fullness and the Protestant one as a search for purity.[5] I am inclined to believe that Catholicism and Protestantism differ still more in terms of temperament and the manner by which believers receive and come to their religion—in being a religion of life, and of life in its fullness, on the one hand, and a religion of searching, of purity, of searching for purity, on the other. In this regard, Protestantism is more intellectual than Catholicism. An idea can be pure; reality and life

4. This passage was translated by Christopher Ruddy and first published in *Commonweal* 126 (January 29, 1999): 14–15.

5. Jean Guitton (1901–99), French philosopher and painter; close friend of Pope Paul VI.

are not. Thus this condition of patience must be added to the first condition [for reform] that I have set forth: a subordination of the intellectual and the systematic to the pastoral.

Heresy comes, in large part, from a purely intellectual grasp of a single aspect [of doctrine]: a grasp which easily becomes an impatient one, freeing itself from the delays of life and from the lengthy schooling of living perception. The mind easily grasps a one-dimensional truth, but an idea, in the process of life in being held and sustained by the life of a man or woman, in finding itself in contact with the questions and conditions of life develops with time other aspects, which a dialectical spirit could not have grasped on its own. Accordingly, there is an immense difference between a truth perceived solely by the mind, dialectically, and a truth matured in solitude or in faithful service, a truth that one has long carried within oneself and nourished with one's life. A too-rapid formulation — the fruit of a purely dialectical intelligence — yields a dried-out product of little inner substance.

The whole work of life, at least here on earth, presupposes delays which do not allow themselves to be breezed over or put aside. Only what has been done with the collaboration of time can conquer time. If certain decisions or changes are to be taken, it is essential that time reveal what meaning certain events concealed, what was to become of certain possibilities, whose mysterious character — often very disturbing — it may have been impossible to guess. For example, many Catholics thought, in the last third of the nineteenth century and the first quarter of the twentieth, that the Holy See might do well to relinquish its temporal possessions. In 1927, when the Lateran Treaty was signed, it seemed to them a true liberation. But, could one have foreseen, in 1870, the consequences for the Holy See's freedom of this loss of sovereignty? Surely, many nineteenth-century Catholics had maintained that a Church untangled from such temporal matters would be more free for action in the world. The future proved them right.

However, others, to whom one cannot deny some perspicacity, predicted that the loss of temporal rule would be the ruin of the Church. Time revealed the groundlessness of this position. But it was legitimate to ask whether the independence of the Holy See would be seriously damaged, and thereby one understands why the responsible powers refused to follow immediately the prophets of a freedom based on the absence of territorial guarantees.

In reality, all reform is a small anticipation of the eschatological kingdom, of its justice and of its purity. Either by their judgment and condemnation on history and its inadequate achievements, or by their constructive movement toward realizing a state of affairs approaching greater perfection and purity, revolutions and reforms are like partial anticipations of the apocalypse. The reformer is always tempted not only to begin development, but to hurry it; not only to clear the field, but to want it free from all weeds. But the Gospel parable teaches us to respect the delays in the growth of the seed and the harvest, and not to encroach upon this by an impatient search for purity, "for fear that with the weeds one also will tear out the wheat" (Matt. 13:29).

There is no better way to end this section on Congar's ecclesiology than with the short conclusion to his 1964 book, Power and Poverty in the Church *(Baltimore: Helicon, 1964). Nothing makes clearer that Congar's academic work is in the service of the community of faith, the everyday life of people, especially the poor.*

I am very conscious of the inadequacy of these few pages in comparison with the holy cause announced in my title. I have been able to approach only from afar, from the outside, and from one particular angle the problem (or rather the mystery) of a Church imbued with the Gospel ideal of poverty. God willing, and granting me courage and strength for the undertaking,

I would wish one day to put forward in all humility some reflections on what is the basis of the biblical attitude of faith, and the very heart of the beatitudes: "Blessed are the poor in spirit!"

Everything that I have said so far shows that several styles have followed one another in the Church's visible presence in the world. No single formula can exhaust the relations of the spiritual with the temporal; none of the forms taken by these relations fully expresses the reality of a Church whose substance escapes time, being of a different order from the things of this world. The Church makes full use of the possibilities that history offers her to live and work in the world; but because she is not of the world she reserves the right to lay aside what has served her for a season and to use other means or give other expression to her life.

Nowadays she is called upon to find a new style for her presence in the world. A presence founded on prestige, exercising an authority whose superiority was acknowledged even on the level of law, may have been acceptable and indeed required in an age of unanimity in religion. When no other voice but the Church's taught men how they should walk, no other arm but hers upheld them, they accepted her not only as the messenger of Jesus Christ but, within the structure of society on this earth and at the very apex of its social organization, as an authority endowed with privileges, splendor, and the means of action that befitted her station. But now men have taken over the ordering of the affairs of the world and become so engrossed by them that they can no longer find interest for anything else. The world has lost the spiritual unity of ancient Christendom; it is divided, and its divisions are in all probability final. Moreover increased production of the means of comfortable living involves men in such relentless competition, intricate organization, and stimulation of appetites and compulsions that even as they become kings they are in danger of losing the health that was theirs in a less affluent and exalted position.

Confronting this world, or rather surrounded by it, the Church finds herself in a situation which must be recognized not only as one historical situation among others, neither better nor worse than others, but also which conforms much more closely with the law of the Gospel; she is called upon to make a clean break with the old forms of her presence in the world, legacies from the days when she controlled the hand that bore the scepter, and to find a new style of being present to men. Individual initiative and spearhead groups which have made their appearance in every country have already clearly outlined the shape of this new style; now it must be given recognition, some sort of consecration on the scale of the universal Church, and urged in the strongest terms at the next [*i.e., the fourth and final, Ed.*] session of the Council.

I was able to say that the present situation of the Church is in closer conformity to the law of Christian life first, because of the distinction and tension between the Church and the world, which was weakened, if not effaced, by the regime of Christendom. And by the same reasoning, because she has been free from the dangers of an association or symbiosis with temporal society which tempted the clergy to adopt the attitudes of the world, not to be ashamed to speak the language of the world or to wear the world's tawdry livery of tinsel and gilt. In a world that has become, or has become again, purely "worldly," the Church finds herself forced, if she would still be anything at all, to be simply the Church, witness to the Gospel and the kingdom of God, through Jesus Christ and in view of him. That is what men need, that is what they expect of her. In fact if we listed all their most valid claims on the Church we should find that they amounted to this: that she be less *of* the world and more *in* the world; that she be simply the Church of Jesus Christ, the conscience of men in the light of the Gospel, but that she be this with her whole heart.

The characteristics of this style of her presence in conformity with the Gospel are outlined in the Acts of the Apostles and the other writings of the New Testament. They can be reduced to three terms, compact with the greatest spiritual meaning: *Koinonia, Diakonia, Marturia* (Fellowship, Service, Witness).

The World Council of Churches has made these three terms the foundation, as it were the tripod on which its program of action stands, and by so doing has gone straight to the heart of truth in its most authentic form. Every initiative inspired by the Gospel leads instinctively in this direction. The ground has been so well prepared, so many appeals are being made to us, that this is the moment for the whole Church to find the new style of her presence in the world by establishing, nourishing, and inspiring true communities of brothers, projects and associations for service, and acts of witness.

These three supreme realities could be the starting point of a positive program of Christian life in the world. The demands they make would not only affect individuals, but the Church herself, *qua* Church, and hence at the ecclesiological level. These three are the sure guides to Christian life; but what part have they in our treatises on the Church? To read them, it seems as if the Church could very well do without Christians and without the life of the Gospel.

A positive program of this kind entails examination of various forms or attitudes which may in some degree betray the Church. To be honest, we are often more sinned against than sinning in our acceptance of these. We come into an inheritance not lacking in grandeur and titles of respect, but which is now so archaic, rigid, and ponderous that we risk being incapable of being *to men* what men themselves and what the Gospel require us to be today. In the outward forms we have inherited from a venerable past we must be ruthless critics of anything that may on the one hand betray the spirit of the Gospel, and on the other, of anything that may isolate us and set up a barrier between us and men. Certain forms of prestige, certain titles or insignia, a certain protocol, certain ways of life and dress, an abstract and pompous vocabulary, are all structures that isolate us, just as there are structures that humiliate or degrade. What was formerly in place in a world much more stable than ours and imbued with respect for established honors is today only a sure way to isolation: a barrier to what we most sincerely desire to express and communicate. Forms designed to inspire respect, to surround us with an aura of mystery, still persist, and their effect today is the opposite of what one would wish. Not only do they keep men at a distance from us, they keep us at a distance from men, so that the real world of their life is morally inaccessible to us. This is extremely serious. For it means that we are in fact no longer able to meet men on the ground where they are most themselves, where they express themselves freely, experience their most real sorrows and joys, face their true problems. We are in danger of living in their midst, separated from them by a haze of fiction.

Naturally, our effort should reach down to include spiritual habits or images which themselves depend, at a still deeper level, on the ecclesiology that we profess at least in practice. We are still a long way from reaping the consequences of the rediscovery, which we have all made in principle, of the fact that the whole Church is a single people of God and that she is made up of the faithful as well as the clergy. We have an idea, we feel, implicitly and without admitting it, even unconsciously that the "Church" is the clergy and that the faithful are only our clients or beneficiaries. This terrible concept has been built into so many of our structures and habits that it seems to be taken for granted and beyond change. It is a betrayal of the truth. A great deal still remains to be done to declericalize our conception of the Church (without, of course, jeopardizing her hierarchical structure), and to put the clergy back where they truly belong, in the place of member-servants. Much remains to be done before we can pass from the simple moral plane where as individuals we act in the spirit of humility and service, albeit within structures of caste and privilege, to the plane of ecclesiological concepts. According to St. Paul, ordained ministers in the Church are the joints or nerves on which the whole of the active body relies for its smooth working (cf. Eph. 4:16); their role is "the perfecting of the saints" (that is, of the faithful) "for the work of the ministry" which is laid upon us all, whose end is the building up of the Body of Christ (v. 12).

We are still a long way from the goal!

To help us make the readjustments that are needed, to give us better understanding of what is at stake, to point the way to new forms of expression and presence in the world, nothing can be more useful than frank exchange of views between the Church and the world, between the Church and other Christians, and within the Church between clergy and laity, circumference and center, parish priests and theologians or specialists in the different disciplines that have something to contribute on this problem. It is in discussion that each finds the truth of his existence; it is the pooling of resources that gives the impetus needed to meet all the demands of one's personal convictions. For the Church, as for every one of us, health consists not only in being herself, but in working out in her life the truth of her relationship with others. A Church thus open to free discussion will be a Church of poverty and service too, a Church which has the word of the Gospel to give to men: less *of* the world and more *for* the world! —PPC 135–41

3

Congar and the Laity

Congar's greatest contribution to ecclesiology was in his focus on the role of the laity in the Church, and his biggest book on this topic was the monumental Jalons pour une théologie du laïcat, *originally published in French in 1954 and appearing in English in 1957 under the title* Lay People in the Church: A Study for a Theology of the Laity, *revised in the early 1960s at the time of the Second Vatican Council. This set of "sign-posts" (French "Jalons") runs to some 450 pages and would be a magnum opus for almost any other theologian, but Congar himself never saw it as anything other than preparatory to a major ecclesiology that, in the end, was never written. A theology of the laity, he thought, is going to be a total ecclesiology. You can't theologize about the laity without it having implications for reflections on the Church as a whole. Here is one brief passage from the opening of the book where he talks about the public role of the laity in world and Church, and the need for a theology of the laity.*

In an essay called "The Layman in the Pre-Reformation Parish," published forty years ago in a Catholic Truth Society pamphlet, Cardinal Aidan Gasquet relates the anecdote of an inquirer who asked a priest what was the position of the layman in the

Catholic Church.[1] "The layman has two positions," answered the priest. "He kneels before the altar; that is one. And he sits below the pulpit; that is the other." The cardinal adds that there is a third that the priest had forgotten: the layman also puts his hand in his purse. In a sense that is still so, and always will be so: there will never be a time when laymen and laywomen are not on their knees before the altar and sitting before the pulpit, and for a long time yet they will have to put hand into purse. Nevertheless, now and for the future they do these things in a different way; or at least, doing these things, they feel differently about their position as a body in the Church.

According to Arnold Toynbee, a proletarian is not made by being in a subordinate condition, but by living in a society of which he does not feel himself to be organically an active member, with his own rights. Laypeople will always be a subordinate order in the Church; but they are on the way to the recovery of a fuller consciousness of being organically active members thereof by right and in fact. We can see signs of this everywhere. It is sufficient to recall the world congress for lay apostleship held at Rome in 1951, in which the present writer had the happiness of taking part as an "expert," along with the representatives of seventy-two countries and thirty-eight international organizations. It is hardly possible to imagine a more telling expression of the fact that something has happened during the past few decades, namely, a veritable rediscovery of the crucial truth that laypeople are fully "of the Church."

To mark the stages of this rediscovery would mean writing the inner history of the Church for the last hundred years. First of all there were the great nineteenth-century leaders, with the first ideas of what was to become Catholic Action. Nearer our own time there was the double movement, liturgical and apostolic or missionary, which is still expanding in all directions. With a return to liturgical sources people here and there began

1. Aidan Gasquet (1846–1929), Benedictine monk and historical scholar who was made a cardinal in 1914.

more and more to realize that the laity is indeed that *plebs sancta,* that consecrated people, of which the canon of the Mass speaks, and that this people has an active part in public worship, the central act of the Church's life. It is in the liturgical movement that we first find a renewed consciousness of the mystery of the Church and of the ecclesial character of laity. There followed a renewing of the theology and spirituality of marriage thanks to which marriage was seen, above and beyond the juridical dispositions that regulate it, as the formation of a cell of the Church.

In the field of apostolic expansion of the Church, the faithful were at the same time rediscovering both the great dignity and the demands of the Christian obligation. They heard the pope and their bishops invite them to "take part in the hierarchical apostolate," that is, in that sacred activity — and not in something else — which defines the Church's proper task and mission; they regained consciousness that they also have a responsibility to tell the world about the Savior, to themselves cooperate in the work of Christ and his Church. To be complete, still more things would have to be referred to the renewed interest in mysticism, the demand for religious books, the importance given to holiness lived in the world, the return to the Bible; and, as regards the clergy, the momentous beginning of a change in the matter of clericalism and clerical attitudes. Such are the main components of a history which we are living in, and so of a history which we are making....

But beside this history which is internal to the Church there is a whole historical and human context which would have to be brought out too, for movements in the Church, and even in theology, are not unconnected with the general movement of ideas and of the world. Such expressions as "The laity has come of age," or "arrival of the masses" are not very acceptable: they belong to realms of ideas different from those with which we are concerned here; they have not much meaning in the Church, so we will not use them. But there are analogies from one field to the other, and even a certain solidarity. And anyhow the development of Christian action by the faithful, and the theological research that goes therewith, is now a general fact in the Christian world, even among those who are not Catholics.

Arising from all this, and in a wide context of ecclesiological renewal, the need for a theology of laity becomes more and more evident. Having sometimes spoken or written a little on the subject, the writer of these pages is repeatedly asked on all hands to speak and write more about it. Not that good books are lacking. The past thirty or forty years have seen the appearance of excellent works, on liturgical life, on marriage in Christ, on Catholic Action, on the Church and the Mystical Body, on lay-people's Christian responsibilities. But for all that many people are still hungry. There is still a void clamoring to be filled.

—LPC xi–xiii

After this introduction Congar launches into a lengthy discussion of the distinction between laity, clergy, and religious, making clear that far too often in Church history the laity have been defined negatively as neither clergy nor religious. He then offers a positive reflection on lay life through exploring the notion of secularity or, in a French term that translates only clumsily into English, "laicity."

The layman then is one for whom, through the very work which God has entrusted to him, the substance of things in themselves is real and interesting. The cleric, still more the monk, is a man for whom things are not really interesting in themselves, but for something other than themselves, namely, their relation to God, whereby he may be better known and which can help toward his service. This parallel could be prolonged with the aid of those passages wherein St. Thomas Aquinas contrasts the points of view of the philosopher and the *fidelis*. The philosopher, that is, the man of learning, is interested in a thing's own nature, the *fidelis* in its transcendent reference; the philosopher seeks the explanation of things, the *fidelis* their meaning. The subject could be carried further by looking in history for types and movements representative respectively of the attitude of the *fidelis* and that of the learned man, in other words, of the cleric and of the layman....

The clerical condition as we have described it is full of danger. First of all, so uninterested an attitude toward earthly things as such commands respect only when it is genuine and uncontaminated, especially in a world so concerned with sincerity as ours. Everybody respects Father de Foucauld.[2] But there is great danger that an attitude adopted in the name of one's state, one's calling, should be too theoretical; that one should lay claim to its honor and benefits without having its spirit or taking up its burdens. And the scandal becomes glaring if a man claims to be disinterested toward the process of history and of the world, when he is really seeking power, wealth (in any of its forms, which are many), advantageous influence in secular things.

That, however, is not the biggest danger. That lies in a loss of respect for the true inwardness of things. The man concerned with the transcendent relationship of things with their principle and end, the *fideles,* and more especially the cleric through his profession, runs the risk of forgetting that things exist in themselves, with their own proper nature and needs. The temptation is to make these things simply occasions or starting points for an affirmation of the sovereignty of the Principle, or as mere means toward the carrying out of some religious program. When earthly disinterestedness is total, when it is truly a matter of pure religious relation, such attitudes, though perhaps still irritating, have something about them that is not only religious but unexceptionable. In the concrete, however, the religious relationship is actualized in a Church, through the ministry of churchmen. Church and churchmen have a historical, sociological existence, and for religious ends they make use of means borrowed from historical and sociological life. The

2. Charles de Foucauld (1858–1916), Catholic priest, missionary, and martyr. He lived as a hermit in the desert of North Africa, seeking to emulate the "hidden life" of Jesus when he lived as a carpenter in Nazareth.

danger, then, is of withholding full respect for earthly human things on the ground that they are being given a transcendent reference, whereas concretely they are simply being used among the sociological and historical means of the Church — as when they are referred and made subservient to "accepted ideas" more than to the faith, to the conventions of "the Christian world" more than to the requirements of Christianity, to the "politics" of Catholicism more than to its mystery. From the minute the historical Church is thought of in this way we go from one thing to the other on the temporal plane without hesitation or discrimination. Perhaps, even certainly, this is a sign of the Church's transcendence; but there is also unquestionably a danger that the temporal engagement should not be treated seriously, and that the nature and truth of the earthly things that compose it are not fully respected. This is particularly serious when it is a question, not of practical action, whose truth is less objectively determined, but of objective truth. In that case any sharp practice "in the good cause" is a betrayal that no apologetic or allegedly apostolic advantage can excuse.

Historically, the Christian regime of the West after the dissolution of the Roman empire, and especially from Charlemagne till the coming of the modern world, which began during the last third of the twelfth century, had its age of power, spiritually, at the Renaissance, politically, after the French Revolution and is not yet over. This Christian regime, "Christendom," was marked by the organization of the whole of temporal life under the supreme regulation of the Church and in her setting; and this meant that all relative realities were brought under tutelage. It is not part of our present purpose to set forth the benefits that accrued to human society from this state of affairs, nor to examine the theoretical question of relations between the temporal and the spiritual. We will simply note two points. (1) In this regulation of earthly matters — the sciences as well as civil affairs — by religious authority, interpreter of the absolute, there was an element of confiscation or, to use a Marxist word, alienation. This alienation was never complete, these earthly matters always had a relative autonomy; but, having been taken into the service of the faith, they were never considered and developed for their own sakes. (2) Guardianship is good for children; but it was unduly prolonged in fields wherein men had, as we now say, come of age. The most typical example — which the clergy can never think about too much — is clearly that of Galileo, threatened with torture when he was seventy years old and made to retract in a scientific matter, and when he was right: this in the name of Revelation — but actually in the name of certain "accepted ideas" which were taken for revealed truth and sound philosophy.

It is against the confiscation of the internal truth of second causes by the First Cause that modern laicism rebelled; fundamentally it was a movement to recapture rights in second causes, that is, in earthly things. The various priesthoods of second causes rose against the alienation of their domain into the hands of the priesthood of the First Cause. A superabundance of proofs could be adduced that this is the true, profound meaning of the lay movement — and of the modern world too. But are any proofs needed when the evidence is so clear? It would be embarrassing to have to choose among all the statements of leaders in the priesthoods of second causes — statesmen, philosophers, scholars, medical men, philanthropists. The following passage from Lavisse[3] has often been quoted:

> To be secular [*laique*] is not to make the best of ignorance about anything. It is to believe that life is worth the trouble of being lived, to love life, to refuse to look on the world as a "vale of tears," to deny that tears are necessary and beneficial, that suffering may be providential; it is not to make the best of any unhappiness. It is not to leave feeding the hungry, giving drink to the thirsty, righting injustice, consoling the sorrowful, to a judge seated outside of this life: it is to join battle with evil in the name of justice.

3. Ernest Lavisse (1842–1922), French historian.

Forget the mockery and the irreverence: it is accidental and peripheral to the meaning and essential intention of the words. The real affirmation is this: to be secular is to use all the resources within us in that pursuit of justice and truth for which we hunger, the very stuff of human history. —LPC 19–22

After the publication of Lay People in the Church *the subject of the laity was never very far from Congar's thinking, and as the years went by he wrote frequently about the nature of the lay vocation, the relationship between the ordained and baptismal priesthood, the apostolicity of the lay role and the contribution that laypeople could make to Church reform. Some of these texts remain somewhat technical; others are much more directly pastoral in tone, a note that became increasingly evident in Congar's writings after Vatican II. In many ways the freshest of Congar's writings on the Church are to be found in three essays gathered in a book with the English title of* Laity, Church, and World (Si vous êtes mes témoins, *Paris: Cerf, 1959*). *A reader today who did not know better would surely swear that Congar was addressing the ecclesial challenges of the twenty-first century, and so in a way he is. Here are some passages from the second and third of those essays (the first will be quoted in the final section of the book under Congar's writings on the Holy Spirit).*

It is clear that the laity are not in the same situation today as they were fifty or sixty years ago. There has been no change in essentials, of course: the Church today is the Church of all time. But the Church *of all time* is the Church of *today* in that she adapts her forms of life and activity to the requirements *of today*. . . . —LCW 35

Where belief is concerned, things are very much changed from what the Fathers tell us about the end of the fourth century. In those days, anybody and everybody used to discuss abstruse questions about the doctrine of the Holy Trinity; a man could not take his shoes to be mended without the cobbler talking about "substance" and "hypostasis." In a famous article, Newman displayed an impressive collection of evidence showing the part played by the laity in safeguarding the true Trinitarian faith throughout the great crises over the Arian heresy; and he remarks elsewhere: "In all times the laity have been the measure of the Catholic spirit; they saved the Irish Church three centuries ago, and they betrayed the Church in England. . . . "

—LCW 36–37

This is a very real aspect of the part that the laity plays; but it must not be exaggerated, nor made into something independent, as if the laity were the only people in the Church. I will try and put it in perspective in a minute. But it is quite certain that, when laypeople are kept in tutelage and treated more or less as children, they become as indifferent to the Church's faith as to her life. Let me give you an illustration from history. In the Scandinavian countries the Protestant Reformation was introduced easily and without upheaval. In 1637 a Norwegian-born Catholic priest, calling himself John Martin Rhugius, came secretly to Larvik in Norway. In the country parts he met people who, a hundred years after the Reformation had begun, did not know that any religious change had taken place; they had noticed that their pastors had altered a number of things, but they thought this was in accordance with orders from the pope for "all over the world."

That was a bitter harvest of the medieval practice of too easily talking about "implicit faith" where the simpler faithful were concerned; this led to the famous "faith of a charcoal-burner" that the Reformers criticized so severely. It is a sort of religion by proxy, in which somebody else thinks and decides for us. Submissiveness to our bishops is absolutely necessary; but it is obvious that a Church made up of Christians who are wholly passive, even from the point of view of belief, will be but a listless, anemic Church. The good health of the Church requires that the faithful be active, even if (as we see in families and schools) robustly healthy children are a bit more difficult to keep in hand than those who are ailing and spiritless.

Today especially, what are wanted are conscious Christians, whose faith is alive and personal, penetrating their whole being. If Father Mersch[4] be right when he says that "some animals need a shell because they have not got a skeleton," then surely Catholics need to be given a strong spiritual skeleton, for all around us the old sociological frameworks of Catholicism are being questioned and weakened by modern conditions and events. If Christendom is to be renewed for its task today, it is no good looking for external supports, government favor and the like, that are no longer there; we have to start from personal conviction, from the witness and influence of men and women who are Christians through and through. In a word, we need people who know and cling to their faith as something living and personal.

Having come so far, I must touch on this question: How is this function of the laity with regard to the faith to be thought of from the standpoint of sound doctrine concerning the Church? The answer—like the answer to a number of other questions—depends on our giving its right sense and meaning to the word "Church." This may surprise you; you may think everybody always does that. I am not so sure. I make it a habit, every time I meet the word "Church" in writings new or old, to ask myself what sense is given to it here, what meaning lies behind it. Try it for yourself, and you will find that perhaps nine times out of every ten the word "Church" in fact signifies the hierarchy of bishops, the governing body, sometimes even simply the pope, with or without the Roman congregations. As if a body consisted only of its controlling organs, or a people of its government ministers and senior civil servants!

No! The Church is a body that is living in all its parts; wholly vitalized by its soul, and that soul is the Holy Spirit. The laity too have the Holy Spirit. But the soul does not animate all parts

4. Emile Mersch (1890–1940), Belgian Jesuit and theologian.

of a human body in the same way, because those parts are differently placed and have differing functions; my soul animates the cells of my skin that it may live and feel, the cells of my brain that it may be an organ of thought and control of movement, and so on. So it is with the Church's members. Spiritual vitality is given to them all: it is given to some simply that they may live, grow, and show forth Christian life; to others, that they may lead and guide.

And there is constant give and take between these and those, in such a way that there is living contact between the life of the first and the direction given them by the second. For they, the laity, are not directed from outside, mechanically, like a stick that is used by a man: direction comes from the organs of a body of which they too are members, whose one life they all share, and they contribute actively to that life, every one in his own place. Thus, just as my mind "takes in" the sensations felt in my skin, so the governing organs of the Church absorb the thoughts and feelings of the whole body of the faithful — without, of course, becoming merely an echo of them....

—LCW 37–40

When we turn to consider Christianity's influence in the life of this world we must not think only of politics in the narrow sense: we must look at the whole of public life, at social legislation, at the way technology is used, at the undertakings to spread and deepen culture, at the general atmosphere in which human beings have to live: in other words, at the whole this-worldly setup.

The nineteenth century produced some notable lay champions of the Catholic cause, and not always without distrustful reactions from some of the clergy. One bishop, for instance, asked by what right Montalembert[5] busied himself in the Church's concerns; and early in the present century an intransigent French editor wrote: "It is for the Church to defend the laity, rather than for

5. Charles Forbes René de Montalembert (1810–70), French historian.

the laity to defend the Church. The Church is the strong man armed, the shepherd standing up to the wolf" (incidentally, notice this example of the word "Church" used to mean the hierarchy without the lay faithful).

These are extreme cases. What seems to me a more common nineteenth-century attitude was to count on the gentry and other big people who were influential because of their social position. Pope Pius IX himself said it was necessary to have an effect on "il Governo." The foundress of the Cenacle nuns, Blessed Teresa Couderc,[6] is an instructive case. She came of farming stock and established her society to teach school, conduct retreats for women, and other work. After a time the priest director decided that a religious congregation of that kind ought not to have a "daughter of the people" at its head, and a widowed countess was appointed in her place; Mother Couderc was allowed to sink into obscurity until her death (but at least she was not turned out of her congregation, as happened to certain other foundresses).

This happening is characteristic of an age that had not yet learned the truth of what Lamennais,[7] for all his extravagances, had had the merit of seeing clearly, namely: that what had formerly been done for religion by the great ones of the earth was now devolving on the people as a whole, that it was public opinion that "got things done"; and that for the future it was these new rulers who had to be turned to. Today, Catholic activity directed toward keeping or making social life Christian is no longer the responsibility of a few important people; it is a ramifying activity whose organizations are spread all over the world. What exactly is this activity in relation to the Church's mission? What is the laypeople's part in it, and so, ultimately, their part in the area of the Church's mission that this action represents?

---

6. Teresa Couderc (1805–85), founder of the Cenacle nuns.

7. Hugues Felicité Robert de Lamennais (1782–1854), a French priest and writer who ended his days estranged from the Church after his liberal views were condemned by the pope.

The Church has existence in herself, of her own; but she does not exist *for* herself. She has a mission, in and to the world: a mission to convert the world, and then, so far as may be, to keep it in the right way, directed toward God and ordered in accordance with his will.

"You must go out, making disciples of all nations. . . . " That is the essential mission, and we have already seen that the laity share in it. For my part, I have always opposed any tendency to insist predominantly, if not exclusively, on influencing the temporal order; apostleship properly so called holds the first place, even where the laity are concerned.

But why should the Church pay attention to secular things at all? For several reasons. First, because faith and charity require it, for they cannot come to terms with just anything that turns up: some states of things are in themselves contrary to love and to faith in God, the Father of all men. Faith and love make demands which can be met in various ways, but they impose a certain minimum and absolutely refuse to condone certain situations.

There is another reason, whose cogency and importance are more and more recognized. Except in rather rare individual cases, people cannot be made Christians unless they have first been "made men." The founder of the Salvation Army wrote: "What is the use of preaching the Gospel to men whose whole attention is concentrated upon a mad, desperate struggle to keep themselves alive? . . . He will not listen to you. Nay, he cannot hear you, any more than a man whose head is under water can listen to a sermon." Or as St. Thomas puts it, "A hungry man is to be fed, not instructed."

Surely that is one reason why missionaries always from the outset join to the proclaiming of the Gospel the starting of dispensaries and schools, improving the condition of women and children, teaching trades and respect for work, caring for orphans and the needy, providing leper and other hospitals. There is thus a sort of "preambles to apostleship," a little like "preambles to faith"; and as the latter are concerned with a certain healthiness of the mind, so the former are directed toward a measure of healthiness of the man and of the social environment in which he has to live and whose pressure he experiences. There is a saying that grace heals at the same time that it raises man up. It is a matter of "giving man back to himself," of restoring his dignity as a human creature made in God's image.

A world consistent with God's will, or at any rate made less contrary to it, can be offered to God, dedicated and turned toward him. This means that, God being Father of all, we must do our best to get rid of everything that fosters antagonism between men and exploitation of one by another, and try to bring about whatever encourages fellowship and service, justice and brotherhood.

By preaching the Gospel, and all that flows from it, the clergy can ensure that this action on temporal things is undertaken. To awaken and strengthen consciences in regard to what is going on in the world, big things and small, is one of the essential duties of the priesthood: for the priesthood in the messianic era has also to be prophetical. But the clergy themselves cannot *carry out* this work: except accidentally and in passing, they are not really engaged in secular life, for they are directly and exclusively committed to the service of God's kingdom. Not for them the two temporal commitments that sum up all the others: the family, through which the human race is carried on, and work in trades, professions, and occupations, by means of which human welfare is provided for.

Laypeople are in a very different position. As I have been trying to show for years, it seems to me that the lay state, inasmuch as it is proper to laypeople, is not a state in which people should seek to serve God and bring about his reign by making as little as possible of their earthly commitment. On the contrary: it seems more and more clear that their state requires them to serve God in and through that commitment. They are married, they have work of one sort or another, they have political concerns, public and social duties, and it is *in and through all that* that they are called to promote God's reign in men's hearts.... —LCW 44–48

[I]t is the laity alone who can carry out this essential (though second) part of the Church's mission, because it is only they who are citizens both of the City that is above and of the earthly city, in whose temporal affairs they are engaged. Accordingly, it is they who have to fulfill the Church's mission in so far as that mission is to influence the temporal order toward God and in the ways of God. In the doing of this, the laity *are* the Church.... —LCW 49–50

Congar next offers a historical sketch of the emergence of a secular world and then asks what the role of the laity is in this new social context:

I cannot go into all the stages and aspects of this process, but the result was the appearance, for the first time in history, of a wholly secular and "unsacred" world, purely of this earth and its time. I say "for the first time in history," because the ancient world of paganism was not like that; it was religious. And we have seen that during the Christian Middle Ages the "city of this world" was as if it slept. But the sleeping beauty has woken up, and she is now very busy. At our work and in our social life we are in constant contact, not simply with Christians who interpret Christianity in a different way from ourselves, but with professed atheists, with agnostics, with those who are puzzled, and with very many who simply do not care one way or the other. We are called to live among and with these fellows of ours, and to witness to Christ's charity before them.

The Catholic Christian may well often feel himself religiously isolated. He is like a soldier parachuted into battle: there he is, he looks about, and he cannot see a comrade nearer than seven or eight hundred yards away, out of earshot. As for the staff officers...? Yet it is the Christian's duty to be where he is. If he chooses to live cozily rubbing shoulders in "Catholic circles," he is then shutting himself up in a sort of ghetto. In addition to the fact that to do so would be repugnant to him as a human being, for he will want to do his bit in the world, he would in that case cease to be a witness to Christ. On the other hand, if he wants to cooperate and to witness — what an undertaking!

Let me quote a few words from Cardinal Suhard,[8] which he wrote during the war; they set out clearly and strikingly the pastoral problem raised for the Church by the situation we are looking at:

> I state this as a fact: our peoples as a whole no longer think in a Christian way; there is a gulf between them and the Christian community and, if we are to reach them, we have got to go out from among ourselves and go among them. That is the real problem. Hitherto our efforts have been almost fruitless; our ordinary Catholic Action has proved ineffectual: it is action on behalf of environments that are Catholic (at least by profession), not Catholic Action on behalf of those that are irreligious.

That is the situation, or a situation tending that way, in which Christian witness and influence has for the future to be taken to the world. We are a long way from Theodosius and Charlemagne, or even Barbarossa! There are no "princes" now; movement has to come from below, not from above, having its source in consciences, not in institutions. If the Church is to fulfill her mission to the world, it is to the laity more than ever that she has to turn: and that is what she has done. Pope Pius XI reiterated that Catholic Action, lay activity, was the answer to worldwide secularization. The laity's hour has indeed come.

In these conditions, laypeople turn to their clergy — for, to the best of my knowledge, the lay advance has not once been accompanied by any undervaluation of the priesthood; on the contrary, it is characterized rather by appeals to the clergy

---

8. Cardinal Emmanuel Suhard (1874–1949), archbishop of Paris, and a major supporter of the Worker Priest movement.

for assistance. Laypeople who want to be witnesses to Jesus Christ in a divided, secularized, non-Christian world turn to us, their clergy, asking to be strengthened with truly spiritual nutriment, I am not imagining this; I have heard them, many times, speaking to this effect:

> Your sermons no longer meet our needs. Religious books are often simply unreal. They seem to be about some sort of life midway between heaven and earth. We are living on earth; but we want to live there really according to the Gospel: not some popularized Stoicism or Platonism, but the full Gospel and the spirit of the Beatitudes. We want to be taught a biblical, evangelical religion, nothing complicated, but something sturdy that will enable us to take on ourselves the burden of our world in a spiritual, a Christian way. "Our world" means the world as it is, as the past has made it and as we have inherited it from that past. There is so much that we have got to take on ourselves in a Christian fashion, which implies in a spirit of responsibility, of service, of a changed heart — all the bitter fruits of capitalism and "every man for himself," the world that has emerged from the French Revolution and scientific rationalism, from the Reformation and divisions among Christians, the legacy of Christians' violence and failings, as well as of Christian grace.... And all the present, with its bewildering problems.... We want the Church to help us face all that together, as a band of brothers; we ask our clergy not to give us ready-made answers, but to help us work out our own answers, with whatever difficulty, day by day; to help us to become men and women who are striving to play a Christian part in a world which has ceased to be Christian.

Unquestionably all that shows the need for a new relationship between pastors and people in some respects. I do not mean, of course, in any sense that would deny or disregard the hierarchical ministry of the clergy (that, alas, is what the Reformation did), but in the sense of an organic cooperation between the two. In this connection there has been no little talk in France of bringing about, not simply a "team" of priest and laypeople, but the "clergy-laity *pair.*" I like that expression. I believe it to be right. The idea of a kind of marriage between a bishop and his flock, a priest and his parish, is a traditional one, and it has found a place in canon law.... —LCW 55–58

Thus daily life goes on in conditions of community and give-and-take. It is this mutual give-and-take that I should like to see going on between priesthood and laity. The actual forms that it could take do not matter much, provided that due respect is invariably given both to fatherhood — that is, to authority — and to fellowship in community; a respect that sees in others, not simply an object, but a subject, a person, a grown-up person. What we need is a dialogue, something that takes place between adult and responsible persons, face to face. And dialogue has two enemies: one is monologue, where only one voice speaks; the other is disorder, when everybody talks at once. "God," wrote St. Paul, "is the author of peace, not of disorder" (1 Cor. 14:33).

I am convinced that along these lines there can be found more far-reaching ways of putting the Christian abilities of the laity to work, and thus the possibility of a new springtime for the Church. —LCW 59

In the third of the three talks in this book Congar turns to the role of the laity in the Church's responsibility to evangelize. His first point is that evangelization in the present day requires the participation of the laity.

The Church is not something made once for all; she goes on being made continually. And the reason for this is that her essence is found, not in organizations and groupings or even in the totality of her practicing members, but in men's faith. It used to be said in medieval days that the Church is not the walls but the faithful. It is a question all the time of enlisting and mustering and increasing a people for heaven, a people among whom God dwells and reigns. But, on one hand, mankind is continually renewing and multiplying itself, generation after generation; and on the other, each individual person's will is changeable and needs to hear a never-ceasing call to conversion.

—LCW 60–61

In all this the Church is seen to be essentially missionary. The "time of the Church," that is, the time between our Lord's ascension to heaven and his second coming, from his passover to his *parousia,* is essentially a time of mission and apostleship (cf. Acts 1:7–8); and so it is the time of that word which proclaims and converts. The fulfillment of God's saving design is what has constantly to be kept in the forefront. It is that which governs the word of the Bible, the Christian word. If we study this idea of the word in the sacred Scriptures we see that it is essentially dynamic, "all reaching out toward the future," as a German writer has put it.

Responsibility for proclaiming the word was entrusted to the twelve apostles. It is of them that it was written — notice the precision and sufficiency of the words — "He appointed twelve to be his companions, and to go out preaching at his command" (Mark 3:14). But, though it is principally theirs, God's design does not entrust this mission to the apostolic hierarchy alone — else why did Jesus join seventy-two disciples with them, and why did one hundred and twenty disciples receive the Holy Spirit along with the eleven apostles at Pentecost? (Luke 10:1; Acts 1:15).

Antecedently, in the natural order of things, we need other people if we are to make the most and best of ourselves. It is only thanks to others that we can do anything worthwhile, starting with our birth into this world. True enough, I get busy, and I hope not to die without having added something, however tiny, to the world's spiritual resources; but this can be done only on the foundation of what has first been given to me. Thus there is a kind of law of mediation through our fellow humans; and this is even more so in Christianity. For, the Gospel tells us, discipleship necessarily involves a spirit and works of service to others, and the better the disciple the more service; to be a disciple and to be a servant... are bound up together, and they diminish or increase together.

The Gospel therefore ordains that every disciple, every follower of Christ, should in one way or another fulfill the service of transmitting the faith, of being, with and through Christ, one sent to proclaim the salvation that he brings and to bear witness to his love. This is the greatest of all services that can be rendered to others, and it is essential to the building up and growth of Christ's Church.

This has always been a universal duty, as has been eloquently attested by the Fathers in the past and the popes in the present. But it must be admitted that there is less relevant testimony to be found in the period between the Fathers and our own time. During those thirteen centuries there was first the era of medieval Christendom when kings and princes were on the whole the only active laypeople; and then came the age of enfeeblement, during which, with a few very remarkable exceptions, the laity had practically no active concern in the forwarding of God's kingdom: the clergy would have been the last to call on them to do so, or even to recognize that they were able to. I could give a number of examples, but the typical one is that of Mgr. George Talbot, a critic of Newman, who wrote in 1867: "What is the province of the laity? To hunt, to shoot, to entertain. These matters they understand, but to meddle with ecclesiastical matters they have no right at all."

It may, then, be said that history has in general seen three types of laypeople: the worldly type, as known to Mgr. Talbot, which is in fact the most common (No? Tell me, what do people think about, what do they talk about?); the "medieval" type, which seeks to defend the Catholic system and extend its influence, but by rather external methods, even by public pressure and "calling in the police"; and the layperson of Church tradition of whom the oldest documents and the Fathers speak, the type which in its full development attains and surpasses the aims of the layman of medieval Christendom, by other means.

There are still considerable remnants of Christendom here and there, and it is possible that in time to come there may be a new Christendom, very different from the old one; but the fact remains that at present the situation of the world is one in which Christians, and especially really believing Christians, are in a minority. And at this same moment there is also a great shortage of clergy, a tragic circumstance which in certain regions threatens to become catastrophic. But whatever the number of clergy, even supposing it were sufficient or superabundant, there would still be a disproportion, a rift, between Christianity or the Church and the contemporary world. It is not only because of their fewness or unequal distribution that the clergy find themselves at a disadvantage in their efforts to reach people and deliver Jesus Christ's message to them: it is because of the nature of the change that has come over the world of twentieth-century man.

What has happened is the emergence of a profane, "not sacred," world, a world of technology; and inevitably, from the very nature of their sacred calling, the clergy are out of contact with such a world. They were quite at home in a world which, at bottom, the Church had shaped, the forms of whose existence were more or less of the same kind as those traditional in the Church; but this is no longer so. The clergy cannot, or only with the greatest difficulty, be at home in a world that is wholly secular, technological, infatuated with man and his earth. On this Ascension day in the year of grace 1958, people are more interested in Sputnik III than in the Lord whom Christians worship.

It is in consequence of this state of things that the laity's hour has struck. They are called to apostleship, to the mission of proclaiming Jesus Christ, in a new way and on a far wider scale. Pius XI and Pius XII said so, repeatedly. Already, in Rome itself, there have been held two international congresses of lay apostleship, each preceded by preparatory national conferences. It is no longer conceivable that a pastoral session on Evangelization Today should omit consideration of "the laity and the Church's prophetical office." —LCW 60–65

Congar turns to the question of whether it is "doctrinally possible" for laypeople to share in the work of evangelization. He mentions the different roles of conserving and bearing witness to the word, of defining, teaching, and pastoral exhortation. These latter three he reserves to the bishops but, characteristically for Congar, asserts the primacy of conserving and bearing witness over these latter functions. And the laity definitely share in these more fundamental dimensions of evangelization.

Now the lay faithful, collectively and each one personally to the extent that he is a living member of the whole, are also responsible for this conservation and this witnessing. At baptism, the faith is committed to them, as a "deposit" sealed by the Holy Spirit; they become responsible for it when they are given grace and power to be *fideles,* faithful. In former times this was expressed ceremonially in the course of preparation for baptism, by the *traditio symboli,* when they were given the baptismal summary of the faith, and the *redditio symboli,* when each made personal profession of that faith. Baptism finds its completion in confirmation. One of the essential effects of confirmation is that it makes the baptized person a witness to Jesus Christ in the world of men. He ceases to be a child in Christ, living, as little children do, for himself alone; he becomes a man in Christ, with his own place in the world of men and with the mission and the grace to bear witness to his Lord in it, by the profession, or better, the confession of the faith....

We must always be careful rightly to understand in what sense the word "Church" is being used. Very often it is used to mean simply the Church's government, the bishops, what

St. Augustine calls the *praesules Ecclesiae,* the leaders or directors of the Church; and when that is done the Church is being looked at only as an organ of mediation between Christ and mankind. I could give dozens, hundreds, of examples of this. One is enough, and it comes from the German national catechism of 1925.

Q. Why did Jesus found his Church?

A. Jesus founded his Church so that she might lead all men to everlasting bliss.

Q. What does the Church have to do for men?

A. The Church has to teach men, to make them holy and to lead them.

It is plain that the word "Church" here signifies only hierarchical mediation, and that the laity do not form this "Church"; they simply represent the "men" on whom "the Church" acts so as to teach, sanctify, and direct them: in one word, they are *an object* of priestly hierarchical activity.

This is not good theology. In sound ecclesiology the laity also *are* the Church. Time and again lately bishops have pointed out in their pastoral letters that the Church is *all* the faithful united in Christ. Pope Pius XII repeated it several times, notably in his address on February 20, 1946: "The faithful, more precisely the laity, are in the front line of the Church's life. . . . "

The Church is an organic body. On the one hand, each member, each cell of this body is living; on the other, all the members do not have the same function in the body, and so its one single soul, the Spirit of Christ, does not animate all the members for the same purpose and in the same way. Some, the faithful laity (and the members of the hierarchy inasmuch as they are in the first place among the faithful) are given spiritual vitality that they may cherish, profess, and bear witness to the faith. Others, the hierarchy as such, are vitalized that they may guarantee and define the faith, and teach it with authority. But all, complete with their differences, form one single "subject," one single responsible person, and that is the *ecclesia,* the Church. So therefore all organically form a single subject that is responsible where witness and evangelization are concerned, proper allowance being made for the differences between the hierarchical mandate, with its pertinent powers and graces, and the simple responsibility that is common to all the faithful....

—LCW 67–70

All this is grounded in the nature of the Church as an organic body, and in God's "plan" for us; more still, like all things ultimately (for all things have something Godlike in them), it is grounded in what I would be so daring as to call God's very structure. We see that from beginning to end his pattern combines a principle of community with a principle of hierarchy, of ordered ranks. I have shown this is true of the Church by reference to her priestly, kingly, prophetical, and apostolic functions. It could be shown to be true also of human society, from the family community up to the political nation, with all the intermediate groupings, professional, economic, and the rest. Two principles, of hierarchy and of brotherhood, have to work together in harmony. Neither one may be upheld without the other: hierarchy without brotherhood is paternalism; brotherhood without hierarchy is bogus democracy and anarchy. It is rather like what Pascal said of the Church: "A multitude that does not form a unity is a jumble; a unity that does not depend on the multitude is tyranny."

In the end it all goes back to the fact that God himself is at the same time both unity and plurality: absolutely one in nature and perfection, in life and glory, more than one in the three Persons who share fully and completely this nature and perfectness. God himself is hierarchy and fellowship: hierarchy, because the Son and the Spirit proceed from the Father, who is the Principle-without-principle, *Fons Deitatis,* the wellspring of Godhead; fellowship, because the Father, the Son, and the Holy Spirit are one and never energize apart from one another.

There is as it were a kind of concelebration between them; and in every aspect of her life, in apostleship or in faith as in liturgical worship, the Church on earth has to strive to reproduce the transcendent example. —LCW 71–72

Given that it is doctrinally appropriate for laypeople to share in the work of evangelization, is it also practical, and how should the sharing be accomplished?

A first form of the laity's participation in the Church's evangelizing function is their more or less active part in the Church's duty of being a sign of God's kingdom before the eyes of the world. This duty falls on the Church as a whole, but it also falls on each local community, and it is at that level that I want to consider it.

The obligation in question is concerned with the general method of proclaiming the Gospel and drawing people to the faith, which is a method of signs and symbols (see St. John's Gospel). Jesus offered men signs, generally parables and miracles, but also himself in his own person. Under those signs the kingdom of heaven was brought close, and opportunity was given to recognize and accept that approach — or to refuse it: for example the parable of the great supper (Luke 14:15–24) and the miracle of the man born blind (John 9); and there was the sign that Jesus himself is, for "nobody has ever spoken as this man speaks" (John 7:46). According to the way a man reacts to the sign he has encountered, so an attitude begins to take shape within him; either one of good will and welcome which, God helping, will lead to faith, or one of ill will and refusal, which will lead to a stubborn turning-away from God's invitations — such a one "will be unbelieving still, though one should rise from the dead" (Luke 16:31). While Christ was on earth it was in this way, by encountering a sign, that men were enabled to see that the kingdom of God was at hand.

Now that Jesus is no longer among us in human form, it is through the Church that the sign comes to men, and this in very many ways. Exceptionally, there are still miracles; there is the occurrence of holiness great beyond the ordinary; there is preaching that is infused with unusual gifts. Sometimes, the heavens open and the Gospel becomes clear and compelling, as clear, compelling, and alive as when Jesus Christ still walked the earth. But, short of these less common signs, there is also the daily life of the Church, with all her aspects that are open to men's sight, things which are signs to mankind that God's kingdom has drawn near to us, that it is open, awaiting us. I am thinking, for one example, of all those expressions of Christianity in the realm of art and culture — such a thing as that standing sign the cathedral of Chartres, which goes on offering to so many pilgrims the Christian message that can be read in its beauty and its modesty. I am thinking, for another example, of those shining lights of Christian life in common, religious communities. A monastery or convent is a sign; it is a revelation of the kingdom of God, a call to faith and to God's service. Mark the telling words that are carved on the choir-screen at the abbey of Maria-Laach: "I, a prisoner in the Lord, beseech you that you walk worthy of the vocation in which you are called" (Eph. 4:1).

But I am also thinking of communities of laypeople. That society of homes, a parish whose people love one another — there too is a sign of God's grace, a call to Christian living. (A parish often reflects the atmosphere of its presbytery, and the first element of the sign is the brotherliness between the clergy.) Or again, a single Christian home is a sign, with its equal balance of freedom and deference; a good home is a striking thing. All these enter into the great sign which the Church is. Think, too, how a warm-hearted friendliness, a token of true sympathy, a kindly neighborliness, testifies to the charity of Christ. And finally, think of the sign provided by a properly communal celebration of the Eucharist, by a parish at worship. I still feel the impression of supreme conviction in testifying to the faith that I experienced when taking part in the Holy Week and Easter offices in certain Alsatian parishes. When they celebrate thus, united with their priests, united by their priests in a single *ecclesia,* the faithful are indeed *bearing witness to the Mysteries.* The liturgy has an incomparable value for evangelization, provided that the sign is genuine and recognizable....

—LCW 76–79

Let me insist on an important point. When referring to baptism of the newly born, I said that this involved the necessity of a catechesis after baptism. But we must go further than that. When an adult receives faith and comes to be baptized, he has made a weighty choice and undergone a true conversion. Now, one of the formidable consequences of the practice of infant baptism is that the moment of personal conversion is passed over, whether as regards the life of the baptized themselves or as regards the activities, or even the pastoral preoccupations and ideas, of the Church.

There is an extremely serious danger here. The success of religious sects is partly explained by the fact that they call for personal conversion, whereas this call is scarcely heard in the corresponding activities of the Church. The sects make much of "revivalism," that is, they appeal for conversion and little else; the Church imparts her catechesis, that is, instruction, without appealing for conversion....

Is this all going too far? Surely it is not putting too heavy a responsibility on Christians to say that they have a duty, in their personal lives, their activities, and their communities, to show forth the signs or parables of the kingdom of God which are so many calls to conversion, conversion not only of unbelievers but also of themselves and of other Christians. It is indeed incumbent on every Christian to do his part with his fellows to enable the Church to be an evangelizing power in the world. Evangelization means putting before men the fact of Jesus Christ, of his call to them, of his deeds that set them free. To evangelize — you know well enough — is not simply to preach dogmatic truth and obtain the adhesion of someone, who thereafter will turn up at Mass; it is to bring Jesus Christ and his sovereign claims into men's lives, into their real, ordinary, daily lives as well as into those occasions when they are faced by hard and important choices.

I have sketched out a scheme of things that may seem to you a bit unreal. What does it actually involve? It involves taking the moral and spiritual demands of the Christian Gospel very seriously, going well beyond meritorious "practices," which can be used to satisfy systematic Catholic requirements without really answering the calls of the Gospel. It involves taking prayer seriously, and the Cross, and brotherly love in a spirit of humbleness and service; it involves getting at the truth of what we say and do in church, and avoiding mere ritualism, which can be a threat not only to public worship but to preaching, "good works," and other things as well. . . .

Word and sign go together in the Gospel. The sign has its full value only when it is illumined by the word. So we must now turn to the word itself, and here too laypeople have their part. There are several ways of teaching. A backward child may be brought home and taught the elements of religion in the simplest form. A layperson can teach catechism officially, by agreement with the parish priest, or because he has been officially commissioned to do so, a true *missio canonica*. A layperson can study sacred subjects and teach them as scientific disciplines; he can be invited by episcopal authority to be a member of committees that study and work out the implications of doctrine or of pastoral care. Most especially, bishops look for the lay contribution in social matters and in problems set by new techniques, when it is a question of judging and guiding them in the light of the Gospel. . . .

It is clear that the testimony to and teaching of the faith . . . by laypeople can in some respects be more apostolically effective than that given by clergy. To speak of God is our job as priests, and people know in advance that when we speak of him we shall be "on his side." In his *Memoirs*, Leon Trotsky[9] relates how when he was a boy at Odessa he went to a school where

9. Leon Trotsky (1874–1940) was a leader of the Russian Revolution. After breaking from Stalin he was expelled from the Soviet Union and later assassinated by Soviet agents.

many of the pupils were German Protestants, and at the beginning of term all were assembled for a sermon. Young Trotsky was much impressed by the solemn atmosphere of the discourse; but he did not understand German, and he asked his neighbor what the preacher had actually said. The boy replied, "He said what it was proper to say."

Yes, it is like that. We clergy, unless we have a bit of the prophet in us, say what we are obliged to say. But when laypeople speak of God, it is taken for granted that they are doing so because they believe in him, and not because it is their job to do so. There can be a more prophetical quality in their words. Furthermore, being actively concerned in the world's affairs, they are more sensitive than the clergy to its "vibrations." The expressions of the faith that they propound on the cultural plane or relating to human commitments inspired by the faith, are sometimes less well balanced than those of the clergy, but they often have more life and "guts," and a better "tone" too. It is not easy to imagine a Bernanos in a cassock; and few of his writings would have survived the ordeal of scrutiny for a *nihil obstat.*

This is a convenient place to refer to a way, if not of teaching directly, of cooperating in the Church's teaching activity, which is open to laypeople and which in fact they do, thank God, make use of. I mean, asking questions of their priests and bishops, and making known their wishes (not demands).

Long experience of teaching and of intellectual life has convinced me that it is questions above all that bear fruit; they are the living seed. The worth of an answer is the worth of the question that has evoked it. Answers without questions answer nothing, literally: they may be customary ritual words, but they are not the living word — all the life has gone out of it. I respectfully invite my brothers in the ministry to join me in an examination of conscience. We have a means of making our work more fruitful, and our answers too if we are able to reach that far — by being open to questions from anybody, and therefore from the laity. Let me tell you something that I have learned, not by deduction from a general principle but by induction from observed facts. I looked about me and I saw a number of different priests or groups of clergy who were outstandingly effective, and I asked myself what accounted for the special quality of all that they said. The answer was plain: all were priests who lived in close contact with laypeople, "in dialogue" with them, always welcoming their questions.

Not that the laity stop short of asking questions to which they await an answer that is like Athene springing fully armed from the brain of Zeus: "The Church says..." (once again, what exactly does "Church" mean here?). No. When they formulate their problems or their desires they also make suggestions. Answers and standpoints are worked out *together,* with proper give-and-take. So here the clergy have a way of learning (and correlatively, the laity a way of teaching), which appears to me to be very effective wherever it is wholeheartedly carried out. It is noticeable that problems, requests, and suggestions from the laity come with an accent of truth; they are plumb on the spot, genuine. It follows that they are also exacting. It is very different from "what it is proper to say."

I believe that clergy who have experimented along these lines will subscribe to the words of a Provençal priest, a Workers' Catholic Action chaplain: "When I was without laity for three years I had the feeling of an empty priesthood." It was St. John Chrysostom, himself a bishop, who called the laity "the bishop's priestly *pleroma,* plenitude." I believe that these statements, like my well-loved expression "clergy-laity pair," present in figurative form something that is very strictly true.

—LCW 80–85

Finally, Congar turns to an outline of the conditions that are needed if the laity are to be able to share in evangelization in the manner he has suggested:

The first condition is of course a fervent life of the spirit. And, since I am a cleric, you will expect me to say "what it is proper for a cleric to say," to wit, that one must be religious, one must pray, and so on. I may surprise you, but I do say that, and, what is more, I believe it! But I say it and I believe it at a different level from that of edifying moral phrases. I believe it because I believe in the mystery of apostleship, because I believe apostleship is a mystery, giving that word its fullest meaning and all its weight.

Evangelization, the proclamation of the Good News, means nothing less than putting into effect the *sequentia sancti Evangelii*, "the continuation of the holy Gospel." Open your Bible and turn to the most concrete of the four written Gospels, St. Mark's; it starts off, "The beginning of the good news [Gospel] of Jesus Christ, the Son of God," and goes on to tell of the preaching of John, the baptizer and forerunner. But the most profound of the Gospels, St. John's, takes that beginning back to before the earthly history of salvation, back to the bosom of the Father, to whom is ascribed *agape,* the love that gives and from which proceeds the Word. Whether we be clergy or laity, our proclamation, our showing forth of the Gospel means nothing less than to carry forward, to the end of time and the limits of space, that saving Word which was born eternally from the bosom of the Father and began to be heard in time nearly two thousand years ago in Palestine. "The Holy Spirit will come upon you, and you will receive strength from him; you are to be my witnesses in Jerusalem and throughout Judaea, in Samaria, yes, and to the ends of the earth": those words are our commission to carry this work on.

As you see, this is quite a different thing from "Doing propaganda," and quite a different thing from being successful on this earth. The propagandist, the publicity man, is simply doing a job, for which he works out a technique. The apostle lives the mystery of the manifestation of God, lives it in his own poor bodily life. He has to be sanctified before being sent out into the world, cleansed and made holy by the word received in faith, as Jesus sets forth in the Gospel according to St. John. It is not only a matter of being very religious and good; it is more than that. It means becoming a whole human creature for Christ's sake, a human being captured, occupied, possessed, vitalized by faith. Again, when I say "faith" I mean something other and more than a simple profession of the truths in the Catechism (though of course this is included). I mean biblical faith in the living God, boundless, openhearted trust, constantly renewed, that he will rule my life, live his mystery in me and radiate his love through me.

It all comes to this, that evangelization is to show forth God, to enable his light to be seen everywhere. I even venture to put it this way, that evangelization is to live and work in order that God may be God and be recognized as God, not only in himself — he is that, with or without us, and we cannot add or subtract an iota — but in the world. This is what was meant by a second-century Jewish rabbi, Simeon ben Yohai, when he said, "If you are witnesses to me, then I am God" (cf. Isa. 43:12). I will end on that profound saying, commending it to your faithful observance. —LCW 85–87

Almost all of Congar's later works include consideration of the particular place of laypeople in the matter under consideration. But his 1967 book Priest and Layman (Sacerdoce et laîcat) *is the lengthiest direct consideration of the respective roles of the ordained and baptismal priesthoods. Chapter 14 of this work, for example, explores the history of neglect of the lay apostolate.*

The object of these pages is not to study the many immediately practical problems of a genuine lay apostolate, but to illuminate these problems as a whole by considering them more radically, in the light of theology and history. History will not here be traced for its own sake, but invoked because it is indispensable in helping us to a correct diagnosis of the present situation. That is true for our first step, which consists in enquiring *how, in what context, and therefore why initiative on the part of the laity has sometimes been neglected and even unknown.*

It was not so in the first centuries of Christianity, including not only those marked by the constant threat of persecutions, but those which immediately followed the peace of Constantine, which are those of the Fathers and the great councils (fourth and fifth centuries). There were warnings, certainly, to respect order, like that of Gregory of Nazianzus:[10] "Sheep, do not tend your shepherds, do not judge your judges, do not make laws for your lawmakers"; or that of Pope Celestine: "The people must be taught, not followed." But only very exceptionally could one then find derogatory terms or statements of the kind we shall quote from the next period.

The fact was that early Christianity lived, and knew that it lived, in a world which had all its weight and toughness as an earthly world. That world was opposed to Christianity, sometimes with great violence. But even when Christianity had become officially favorable, that world possessed, by its culture inherited from the pagan era, by its political and juridical organization, by its traditions and prestige, a solidity and visibility which did not allow it to be unaware of Christianity as an equal, and so as a rival, even when it had become an ally. While living in that world, the Christians stood, as it were, confronting it. Christianity appeared to them as *something else,* as a life connected with another kingdom, one that is eschatological. Under these conditions clergy and laity, despite the strongly marked inequality of their positions, were more readily aware that they formed the people of God, on the march to its true country, the goal of its pilgrimage.

From the patristic age, however, we find a tendency to express the opposition between the two worlds on the moral level and in terms of ascetic life, as a difference in the quality of Christian life. The historical consideration of a present and a future world certainly did not disappear, but another notion was often superimposed upon it, that of two moral worlds coexisting in this life, a world from above and a world from

10. Gregory of Nazianzus (330–89), archbishop of Constantinople.

below, regarded as a world of the spirit and a world of the senses, in a climate of thought where a platonic view of things was not unfamiliar. It contained the germ of a certain depreciation of the earthly life, a germ which was developed in later ages, so steeped in the monastic spirit.

Yet another cause of the depreciation of the laity began to appear in the classical age of the Fathers. Since the conversion of Constantine, the Church had enjoyed the favor of authority. This favor took the form, among others, of granting privileges to the clergy: bishops, priests, and monks obtained important immunities. A whole series of enactments resulted in distinguishing the priests from the laity, by the type of life (celibacy), the wearing of a special dress copied from the monks (latter part of the fifth century), and so on. The clergy thus stood aloof from ordinary Christians, whose life was considered more carnal.

Another process was soon to operate in the same direction, perhaps even more strongly: the general lowering of culture, the disappearance, total or partial, of schools in the West, subject to the barbarian invasions. The Church, as the only institution to keep its place, vested with the prestige of religion and of Rome, became the sphere where learning and the knowledge of letters survived. Culture became a sort of monopoly of the clergy and the monks. From the late Middle Ages down to the Renaissance, *litteratus* ("one who knows letters," that is, Latin), was synonymous with "cleric," whereas the synonym for "layman" was *illiteratus* or *idiota* (a simple person, one who cannot explain things).

It is not surprising, therefore, to find in the Middle Ages certain signs of what might well be a depreciation of the laity and of their ability to carry out the Church's tasks, signs which have their full meaning in the circumstances we have just mentioned. There is, for example, the distinction between *majores* and *minores,* that is, between those who by their state had more powers and responsibilities and those who had less: the people of above and the people of below (without, in the case of the latter, any pre-Marxist consciousness of frustration). This distinction (while justifiable on practical grounds in the existing conditions of education) tended to give the laity a state of inferiority or tutelage, sometimes accompanied with some contempt and even mistrust with regard to their capacities. The absurd philology which derived *laicus* from *lapis,* on the ground that the laity had minds as hard as stone, did not meet with much success, but innumerable were the texts which likened the laity to the obscure or mean term, in comparisons where the glorious or noble term was applied to the clergy. The clergy were the day, the laity the night; the clergy were the heavens, the laity the earth, or again, the soul and the body respectively; the clergy were like angels or gods, the laity like beasts of burden, *jumenta, laicorum genus bestiale.* Texts were quoted from Scripture, such as Job 1:14: "the oxen were ploughing, and the asses feeding beside them," the *asinae* were the *simplices,* the laity. Or Numbers 22:22: "Balaam was riding on his ass": Balaam represents the clergy and his ass the laity. Or Deuteronomy 22:10: "You shall not plough with an ox and an ass together": this text was sometimes applied to laity and clergy, who should not be put to work together. It is true that this was on the subject of definite judicial functions, but the quotation, in connection with others, is still characteristic, especially when compared with the formulas of today, strongly favoring the association of ox and ass — if that is what they are. It is also true that in the atmosphere of the ideal of organic unity which inspired the Middle Ages, all these comparisons did not have the scornful and insulting sense they would have today: they then signified participation in one whole rather than opposition. Nonetheless they stand as a proof that the laity were allotted a place of minority. . . .

In a Christian society, all of which has become the Church, there is no longer true tension between a Church purely the Church and a world truly the world. Tensions exist, of course: they are everywhere, but they have to do with the interior of the Church. From the end of the eighth century till the time of Gregory VII, the name *ecclesia* was regularly given, in the West, to the whole Christian society, which was both temporal and spiritual, almost without distinction. Even after the Gregorian reaction, which was aimed at escaping from this confusion, the whole Cistercian current of thought, and many authors of more or less theocratic tendency, accepted the identity of the Church and Christian society, in their theory of a Church composed of different *ordines*. Then the tensions were transferred to the interior of this *ecclesia*-cum-Christian society. There was the tension between the clerics and laymen, culminating in the incredible statement of Boniface VIII, calmly announced as if it were self-evident: "That the laity have always been extremely hostile to the clergy is what we learn from antiquity, and what the experience of the present time makes abundantly evident." Then there was the tension between the power of the kings and the authority of the priests, between the secular and regular clergy, even between different Orders among the regulars. These tensions fill the whole history of the Middle Ages, each one representing a paragraph in the chapter of each century's history.

The condition of the laity was to change with the birth of the modern world, of a world, that is, which was really a world, and therefore lay. Up to then, ever since the conversion of the prince who had inaugurated and founded the régime of Christendom, the princes had been practically the only laymen to be active in the Church's service. They were trained to piety in order that they might make laws in accordance with the demands of religion, and in this way a world was maintained in existence which was subject to the commandments of the faith and the directions of the priesthood, or rather, for high and low alike, to its authority. But when the age of criticism began, that is, when men seized their independence in the various fields of politics, science, reflection and research, judgment and criticism, the organization of life and, in short, of the City, a real world was found — or refound — outside the Church and face to face with her. Laymen rose up to take their part in the Church's fight in the various fields where it was waged.

— PL 241–45

What has happened? Quite simply, that there is now a world—and what a world!—which is truly a world, *and that we know it.* For it is not enough for a world to exist: we must know it as such and reckon with it. It could easily be shown that even today, wherever the Church is not faced with such a world, or does not realize that she is, traces are still to be found of those internal tensions, sometimes both futile and petty, which were so evident in the ages of faith. The lesson of history, some episodes of which we have just recalled, is very clear. It will dominate all that we have to say here. History shows that the apostolate of the laity is taken seriously only when a real "world" exists to confront the Church, and the Church is aware of it. Then the tension is felt for what it is, a tension between the Church, seed and sacrament of the kingdom of God, and the world. In those conditions priests and laity feel themselves to be called and yoked to the same task: the laity are no longer mere passengers in a ship navigated by the clergy alone: they are, in their own place, part of the ship's company.

But even today there is still to be found among certain clerics something of the mistrust, low opinion or reserve which was often shown by their seniors toward the initiatives or activities of the laity. The laity, at least, feel it to be so and complain of it. They say they feel that they are not taken seriously when they take part in certain Church matters or merely give their opinions about them.... —PL 247

Congar was of the opinion that depreciation of the laity was a product in part of a deficiency in ecclesiology and in part a deficiency in anthropology. First, the ecclesiological problem.

This is bound up with our admirable and holy Catholic objectivity: the most insidious temptations are not the common, blatant ones, but those that are noble and concealed. Now with [us priests], belief is guaranteed in objectively defined dogma, in the infallible statements of the catechism, the encyclicals, our manuals, our *Denzingers.*[11] The conduct to be followed in almost any circumstances is determined by a whole system of jurisprudence and casuistry: we have only to consult a good author or *L'ami du clergé.* Worship is regulated by precise rites and rubrics: the prayer I am obliged to offer is ruled by an *ordo* printed eighteen months in advance: the administration of the sacraments is prescribed and defined, not only in its liturgical and ritual aspect but as a pastoral action, which derives in turn from a known system of casuistry and jurisprudence.

The grandeur of all this is the objectivity of the order of salvation and the structures of the covenant: it is not for me to make them; I have simply to enter into them, somewhat as in the Scriptures I am invited to "enter into" the kingdom....

But there is a great and by no means imaginary danger that the assurance of the system may let us out of performing, in all this, a spiritual, personal act. We run the risk of treating the faith and worship, and even the ministerial acts for which the faithful resort to us, as ready-made things, of which we are hardly more than mechanical transmitters. We risk seeking to maintain a ready-made system, not committing ourselves by a spiritual, personal act. Many priests... have got into a deeply engrained habit of serving in the first place "the Church," her greatness, her influence, her prestige. In all good faith on their part, this sometimes obscures in their eyes the primacy of persons. They come to see "the Church" herself as the first thing to be served, instead of as the constant recipient from God of all she needs for the service of men. And so they handle "things," which are self-contained and dispense them from looking for the event of a personal encounter with God, with Christ, with the Gospel and its claims, with grace, with prayer.

---

11. Heinrich Joseph Dominicus Denzinger (1819–83) was a leading German Catholic theologian and author of the *Enchiridion Symbolorum,* a handbook of Catholic dogma and theology.

It is God who brings about that event, or rather, the event is simply his coming. So it is free, and can be brought about even through the "things." In itself, however, the event belongs to the order of personal relations. Inasmuch as it falls to us to prepare its ways it requires an intense effort from us to ensure that each of our pastoral acts, whether in the conduct of worship, or preaching, or the various relations with men as priests of the Gospel, may represent so many real *spiritual acts*. By "spiritual act" I mean an act in which I commit myself laboriously, as a spiritual man, offering myself for the action which the Holy Spirit is carrying out perhaps through me, for the good of other men, and which is the right one for encountering them, challenging them, in the sight of God, in the name of the Gospel. This presumes that I commit myself as a religious man, living by the grace of God and under the call of the Gospel....

From the point of view of ecclesiology, what demands such an attitude is the experienced conviction, formulated by an age-old tradition, that it is not the walls, but the faithful, that make the Church; not a system, but men touched by Christ and engaged in personal encounter with the God of the Gospel. If our pastoral work is directed in practice (whatever our intentions may be) to the application, the service, and the reinforcement of a ready-made system, the faithful can only be treated as objects or "patients" of our action, or as material for the power of the Church. If our pastoral work aims at producing real spiritual acts and ensuring that something really happens spiritually, then the faithful are personally involved, and called to commit themselves; they can do something with us: not only when they are the beneficiaries of our ministry, but as members of the ship's company, jointly responsible with us for the voyage, cooperating in the whole pastoral work, for which the priest, under the authority of the bishop, is obviously the one chiefly responsible and the leader, or, to keep to our metaphor, the ship's captain.

It is only on the basis of an ecclesiology which is spiritual, not thing-centered, and a concept of the Church as made of the faithful, not of walls, that we can understand and restore the patristic idea of spiritual motherhood as the function of the whole Church. The texts of the Fathers on this subject are extraordinarily numerous and forcible. To them we must add the witness of the liturgy: we can never comprehend Lent as the liturgy understands it unless we see the work of conversion, which is its aim, as the undertaking of the whole *ecclesia*. In the eyes of the Fathers and the liturgy, as soon as a Christian has been engendered by faith and grace, he engenders others in his turn: and not only by his witness but by his whole Christian life, which is prayer, penitence and charity. Once again, it is a matter of administering "things," the priest is adequate and he can do it alone: he is, alas, the "medicine-man." But if it is a matter of engendering souls to Christ, leading them to God, helping to produce a personal encounter with him, then the laity exercise that spiritual motherhood personally, and the whole Christian community exercises it collectively. The role of the priest is, then, to "organize the saints (all the faithful) for the work of the ministry."

There is a very simple, infallible way to find, in practice, the true attitude. It is connected with the concept of the Church as made chiefly of Christians, for it follows from that, that Christianity has precedence in the Church over whatever is simply system or "things." Augustine constantly repeated to his flock, in this form or some other: "For you I am a bishop, (but first of all) I am a Christian with you." Or again, "Disciple with you, servant with you, sinner with you, beating my breast with you." In the Liturgy of St. John Chrysostom the priest often places himself as it were with the faithful, praying as one of them to receive grace and asking to be forgiven for his unworthiness. Often, even in the Middle Ages, the priest, conscious of his own defects, asked the faithful, before beginning his sermon, to pray for him and with him by reciting the Lord's Prayer, for example.

—PL 249–52

The ecclesiological issue is matched by an anthropological concern.

And so with cosmology: if priests have too little faith in the laity, it is no doubt because they have too little faith in man.... Let us get this clear: it is not a matter of substituting faith in man for faith in God: there must be a high esteem of man and man's work, an esteem whose deepest foundation, I am convinced, is precisely a true theology, that is, a fully scriptural knowledge of the living God, for "the Bible is not a theology for man, but an anthropology for God." Say, rather, that it is both, or better still, that it is the unity of both.

There are many laypeople who accuse us of not having enough faith in man. We often give them the impression that we are carrying out a role, a program of obligations, rather than being at their service, to help them practice, in their actual life, that anthropology for God of which we spoke. It would be very interesting to make a critical study of the anthropology professed and the anthropology implicit in the documents of the teaching authority, and even in the more or less classic authors used in the training of the clergy and the religious orders since the Council of Trent....

Certain priests... practically never get near the sort of men who are fully engaged in the stern competition of the world. They would rather avoid them. They are in contact with some men and women (and children, of course) who belong in some degree to the world of the devout: much religion, not much man. The devout world makes a sort of halo round them which isolates them from the real world of men. They run the risk of never meeting any but people of their own religious world, people like themselves: whereas the real world is very different, very separate from our world, and is becoming increasingly so. In fact our pastoral ministry is very largely one of like to like, In a country like France, at least, where up till now practically all the children have been baptized, been through the catechism and even made their first (often last!) communion, our pastoral ministry has been largely a ministry of recovery, if only *in extremis,* of those who had belonged and still virtually belong to our religious world. A ministry of like to like.

But the world becomes more and more apart and even foreign. It was the realization of this fact that impelled Cardinal Suhard to write in his *Carnets,* during the war "I observe a fact: that our population as a whole no longer think themselves Christian. Between them and the Christian community there is a gulf fixed, which means that in order to reach them we must go *out from our own ground and enter theirs. That is the real problem.* So far our efforts have been almost without result: even our ordinary Catholic Action admits it is helpless: it is an action of Catholic milieux. Catholic at least in belief, it is not Catholic action on pagan milieux." It is clear that this statement of the facts commits us to a pastoral ministry of full witness to the faith in a world which we confront with no safety margin, as one confronts the open sea. Clearly, in this pastoral situation, the relation between priest and laypeople can only be one of full collaboration, of apostolic and missionary action in common. But it also presupposes that the clergy have convictions about man and the world, anthropology and cosmology, which flow from a scriptural faith in the living God! —PL 252–55

One of the most notable and frankly endearing qualities of Congar is his intellectual humility. Time and again in his later life he publicly recognized the mistakes of his earlier writings, nowhere more clearly than in a 1972 article in The Jurist *entitled "My Pathfindings in the Theology of Laity and Ministries."*[12] *In the following extracts you can see Congar coming to terms with knotty issues in his own previous writings and in the challenges facing the Church in the years after the Council. Having said that he will offer "an overall critical examination" of his own contribution to the theology of the laity, he sets the scene with the events of World War II:*

---

12. Spring 1972, 169–88.

Then came the war with its train of fateful events, captivity, the exodus on the roads, the fraternity of distress, the comradeship of the Resistance, all contriving to lead us into the rich but demanding experience of a laity aware of its obligation to active existence in the Church, and to the sense of the immense extent of ignorance of the Gospel as well. The real world of men was much more remote and foreign to the faith than we had thought even after so many searchings. But on the other hand priests and faithful alike had undergone experiences and uncovered tracks which the years of peace had not hitherto revealed. The upshot was that in the euphoric post war years of liberty regained, 1946–47, the question of the status of the laity in the Church forced itself upon us in a new way.

These were the years when Congar was planning his great book on the laity in which he developed the ideas we have already encountered, on the secularity of the laity. As he looks back from this vantage point he wonders if he has been wrong to settle for the priesthood/laity doublet, and suggests instead attending to multiple ministries.

The plural noun is essential. It signifies that the Church of God is not built solely by the actions of the official presbyteral ministry but by a multitude of diverse modes of service, more or less stable or occasional, more or less spontaneous or recognized and when the occasion arises consecrated, while falling short of sacramental ordination. These modes of service do exist. They include, for example, mothers at home catechizing the children of the neighborhood, the man who coordinates liturgical celebration or reads the sacred texts, the woman visiting the sick or prisoners, a parochial secretary, the organizer of a biblical circle, the member of a team of adult catechists, the man or women who acts as secretary to Catholic Action or to an auxiliary movement for the missions. It might even be someone who initiates help to the unemployed, arranges hospitality for migrant workers or someone responsible for the family hearth or for a course in basic literacy. These are just instances of which the last relate, if not to the upbuilding of the Church itself, then to its *diakonia.* Such modes of service proceed from gifts of nature or grace, from those callings which Saint Paul named "charisms" since they are given "for the common good" (1 Cor. 12:7, 11). They do actually exist but up to now were not called by their true name, ministries, nor were their place and status in ecclesiology recognized. To move on to this double recognition is extremely important for any just vision of things, for any satisfactory theology of the laity. As to terminology, it is worth noticing that the decisive coupling is not "priesthood/laity," as I used it in *Lay People in the Church,* but rather "ministries/modes of community service. . . . "

Let us briefly say that Jesus has instituted a structured community which is as an entirety holy, priestly, prophetic, missionary, apostolic; it has ministries at the heart of its life, some freely raised up by the Spirit, others linked by the imposition of hands to the institution and mission of the Twelve. It would then be necessary to substitute for the linear scheme a scheme where the community appears as the enveloping reality *within which* the ministries, even the instituted sacramental ministries, are placed as *modes of service* of what the community is called to be and do.

Congar concludes this essay in typically humble fashion:

Where problems of a currently urgent kind are concerned I wished to make no more than brief suggestions. Their elaboration will be the work of years to come. The world is in the making every day. As is the Church. As is theology. So I am not ashamed to have evolved a little myself nor to be still a researcher. For if we have to seek as though we were about to find, we also have to find as if we were about to seek.

4

Congar and the Spiritual Life

Congar's writings on ecumenism, ecclesiology, and the roles both of the ordained and baptismal priesthood are as radical and far-reaching as anything written in the mid-twentieth century. Yet there is another side to him, one equally important. A learned, adventurous, and sometimes technically demanding theologian, he also evidenced a simple piety and a commitment to traditional practices and devotions. In this regard he was not unlike his exact contemporary, the Jesuit Karl Rahner. Many of Congar's writings, especially the later collections, show him to be a holy man of great wisdom, a man with profound spiritual depth and with a strong pastoral sense. What follow are some passages from these seemingly much more traditional works, texts that will definitely surprise some in their simplicity and traditional piety.

ON THE HOLY ANGELS

The doctrine of the guardian angels and devotion to them belong to the riches of the Church's Tradition. A host of witnesses might be involved here, but I shall limit myself to an answer made by Joan of Arc to her judges; it has such admirable frankness: "Asked whether the angels were wont to stay with her for any length of time, she answered that they often come to Christians without being seen, and that she had seen them among Christians many times." A lively appreciation of this doctrine seems to go hand in hand with an understanding of the great spiritual realities. Unfortunately, the truths of Christianity, which are mysteries, are as difficult to transmit as a secret.

Why is it that the holy angels play so small a part in our spiritual life? One reason, among many others, would seem to be that Christians in general hardly ever read the Scriptures. They feed their devotion with the reading of good books, devotional books, which give them, often at a second or third hand, the teaching of scholastic writers of the sixteenth and seventeenth centuries. In literature of this kind the most living truths of Christianity, even when not expressed sentimentally and as a mere matter of words, are made to appear theoretical and artificial. As a result, the ensuing conviction is equally theoretical, sentimental, and verbal, and lacks that intimate, warm, and strengthening persuasion which Holy Scripture intrinsically promotes.

There is another more general reason for our indifference to the angels: this is the individualism and the moralism of our piety. It is true, of course, that a guardian angel is personally given to each of us, but the very fact that we have guardian angels is the result of a social plan, of salvation thought of in terms of the Church, of a corporate body, a plan and a point of view which has largely been lost sight of in the individualistic and moralistic mentality that has developed since the sixteenth century. Earlier centuries, especially those before the development of strictly scholastic theology, had looked for the sustenance of their piety more to biblical and liturgical sources. From these they gained an acute understanding of the totality in which the mystery of Christ consists, a totality which includes the Church and in which our own salvation is a function not of autonomous struggle maintained by our own strength, but of an action entirely based on what Christ the conqueror has already achieved and supported on every side by the universal

Church. If such ideas seem strange, this is due to the fact that a genuinely Christian understanding of spiritual realities and of the conflict between good and evil in the world is lacking. The ancient and traditional spirituality of the Church is, as Dom Vonier[1] observed, that of the *Te Deum:* the praising of God for the redemption and for Christ's victory, both of which have been achieved, and also the joy of that praise, in which, with all creation, and with the whole Church and the heavenly hosts, every Christian comes to see what life means as a real mutual association between his own happiness and God's glory. This immediately removes the emphasis from personal ascetic effort and from salvation considered exclusively as an achievement due to our own hard-won struggle, to God's regal initiative, to the really universal significance and the full extent of the salvation brought about by God in Christ. A spirituality of this kind is more akin to a truly Catholic appreciation of the supernatural world and of the conflict between good and evil in this world. It is a spirituality in which the angels regain their position quite naturally. In the first place it gives us the joyful realization that in them God finds perfect praise and obedience: "O praise the Lord, ye angels of his, ye that excel in strength: ye that fulfill his command, and hearken unto the voice of his words" (Ps. 103:30)....

Our relationship with the angels and the devotion which we owe them has its roots in the economy of the kingdom of God which gathers them together with us, in a special way, within a single Church. Not that the angels form part of the Church militant on earth as we do, nor that like us they receive God's life from Jesus and through his cross. But we should not forget, first of all, that in heaven a single Church exists, made up of all those who live in fellowship as friends of God: the angels form part of this kingdom of God's saints described by the prophet Daniel, just as men do. Secondly, even with regard

1. Dom Anskar Vonier (d. 1939) was an Anglo-German Benedictine abbot and the author of many books.

to the Christian society, the kingdom Christ won through the cross, the angels have a real part in it with us. It is true, of course, that unlike us they have not been redeemed by Christ's cross, but owing to that cross, they have received a new and holy function, an ennobling ministry: "Are they not all ministering spirits to send forth to serve, for the sake of those who are to obtain salvation?" (Heb. 1:14). On account of this ministry they are to exercise among the redeemed people of Jesus, the angels may be said to come under the influence of Christ, the sole mediator of the new economy of grace, for it is from him that they receive the grace of this new ministry. This fact enables them to be admitted and incorporated into Christ's kingdom, the Church; they have their place in that economy of Christian grace of which Christ is the source, the originator, and the head; they form part of the Christian society as "spirits sent forth to serve"; from this point of view, it may even be said that they form part of the Church militant, somewhat in the way that soldiers serving under a foreign flag, fighting for a land which is not theirs, become an authentic part of the army of that land, and have their share of the commander's inspiration in the common struggle....

It follows from this that the angels are our brethren in the supernatural world, our elder brothers; they watch over us and help us. We ourselves cannot know all the beauty of a soul in a state of grace, and St. John tells us that we do not yet know all that it means to be a child of God (1 John 3:2). But the angels see the full stature of a Christian soul. They who serve God in his intrinsic reality and who worship him, also serve him in us and in us profoundly reverence him. Just as theology is the science of God and remains the science of God when it studies the divine life in us, and just as charity is a theological virtue and remains such when it loves God's goodness as shared by man, so the angels remain God's worshippers and servants when they reverence and serve him in us. It is angel theologians, angels with a theological heart and vision — if the phrase may be used — who have been commissioned to guard us; for in that frail earthen vessel that we are, they guard the treasure of divine life, that hidden seed of glory which is the pledge of our heavenly inheritance. They are commissioned to serve the interests of those who will receive the inheritance of salvation....

There is a further consideration which is of assistance in understanding the purpose of the angels and in stimulating our attention to them: this springs from the fact about which St. Paul cautions us that "we are not contending against flesh and blood, but against the principalities, against the powers, against the world rulers of this present darkness, against the spiritual hosts of wickedness in the heavenly places" (Eph. 6:12). The great conflicts in this world are spiritual conflicts; it is ideas that govern the world and in the great human conflicts opposing gospels are always involved. The slightest deviation in doctrine, so slight as to be almost imperceptible to our crude power of appreciation, can have incalculable repercussions; it can stem the growth of charity in a host of souls. On the other hand, a single soul, a single degree of charity, either more or less, in one soul redeemed with Christ's blood is a spiritual reality incomparably more important than the whole material universe. As Pascal[2] remarked: "all bodies and all spirits together, with everything they produce, are not equal to the least movement of charity, for it belongs to an infinitely more exalted realm of reality." In the spiritual realm, therefore, we must maintain absolute fidelity and integrity, for without that the pure gold of charity will be changed into leaden dross. And if we fail in preserving this spiritual integrity, if we in any way stunt or adulterate the truth, we shall experience one of those distressing falls which only those who have been called to a high degree of union with God can suffer....

It should now be easier to understand why the guardian angels are necessary to us and why we should turn our minds to them often. It should also be easier to understand why a man

---

2. Blaise Pascal (1623–62), a scientist, philosopher, and Catholic apologist, best known for his *Pensées*.

like St. Thomas Aquinas, predestined by God to be theologian of the Church, above all needed to be endowed with that grace which made him the Angelic Doctor. And since, in the Church, there exists an "Order of Doctors" with a special mission to promote purity of charity through purity of belief, it would seem that those whom God calls to such an office in the body of the Church have a special need to be in communication with the angels and to receive assistance from them. Against Lucifer who knows and appreciates the loftiest and most subtle realities and who tries to pervert them, we who are fashioned from the earth and yet must be the lights of the world, most certainly need the angels!

Because the angels give incomparable glory to God, because they are our elder brethren sustaining in us the reflection of God's face, because our real struggle is not against flesh and blood but against far stronger spiritual powers, we should love them deeply and pray to them often. God will ask for an account of how we have appreciated this among his other mercies, whereby he has bestowed on each of us an angel of his face, to help us in our journey back to him. —FSL 11–18

ST. PETER

Catholics are very familiar with the passage in St. John's Gospel (21:15–17) in which the risen Jesus says to Peter: "Feed my lambs . . . tend my sheep. . . . " It is generally agreed that the text expresses the commission to Peter of a *universal pastoral ministry over everything connected with the sheepfold of Jesus*. This is of immense importance. In the lines that follow I shall examine, without any claim to specialist knowledge, the relationship between some passages of the New Testament in order to obtain an idea of the great religious significance of Peter's ministry. The first passage to come to mind in this connection is that on the Good Shepherd (John 10:1–18). Here it is Jesus who is the good shepherd. He is so, in the first place, because he looks after the sheep. For an oriental the idea of a shepherd would almost certainly suggest the thought of almost affectionate care and gentle rule. The prophet Nathan's admirable little parable addressed to David comes to mind: "The poor man had nothing but one little ewe lamb, which he had bought. And he brought it up, and it grew up with him and with his children; it used to eat of his morsel and drink from his cup and lie in his bosom, and it was a daughter to him" (2 Sam. 12:3). The good shepherd is thus anxious for his flock; he is not concerned about himself, he does not take to his heels at the approach of danger, and does not shrink from giving his life for his sheep. In the parable of the good shepherd, Jesus also tells us that he alone is the true shepherd of the sheep, the only one whose voice they hear, whom they recognize and follow.

Lastly, Jesus is the shepherd because he gives his life for his flock; in the same passage in St. John, Jesus expresses this idea twice (10:15 and 17–18); I give my life for the sheep. Between these two verses these famous words occur: "And I have other sheep that are not of this fold; I must bring them also, and they will heed my voice. So there shall be one flock, one shepherd." Inevitably there comes to mind the other passage of St. John (11:52–53) which tells us that Jesus had to die "not for the nation only, but to gather into one the children of God who are scattered abroad." It is through his death that Jesus gathered us together in himself as in his flock; it is through his death, the first act in the great mystery of his passing to his Father (John 13:1, 3, and 16:28), that he was enabled, and we with him, to enter into glory; it is through his death that Jesus gathered his flock together, the flock of redeemed mankind, and that he made himself their gate, their way, their access road to God's pastures. It is through his death that Jesus enabled us to enter into the unity of his sheepfold.

When all this had been achieved, that is, when Jesus had died for his flock, had given his life (John 10:15), and had taken it up again by his resurrection (vv. 17–18), what did he do? He turned to the apostle who had thrice denied him and caused him to confess three times that his love for him was greater than that of the others. He thereupon entrusted him with the universal pastoral ministry over his sheep and lambs; then he who had said that he walks in front of his flock added that he would lead Peter where he willed and that Peter had only one thing to do: to follow him. Thus Jesus is the first leader, the originator, the prince; Peter follows him and the flock of Jesus follows Peter.

We turn now to the first epistle of St. Peter, and note the obvious and very moving echo of these two episodes related by St. John — Jesus as the good shepherd, and the entrusting to Peter of the government of Jesus' sheep and lambs. "For you were straying like sheep, but have now returned to the Shepherd and Guardian of your souls" (1 Pet. 2:25). These words follow a passage that recalls the passion of Jesus, his redemptive passion, deeply felt and detailed. So Peter is thinking of the death of Jesus as effecting the assembly and unity of his whole flock. He reminds us that it is by redeeming our souls with his blood that Jesus gathered us into the unity of his flock, the sheepfold of the redeemed, of which he is the gate. It seems indeed that the consciousness of their pastoral responsibility was connected in the minds of the apostles with their memory of the cross, as is evident from St. Paul's advice to the elders of Miletus: "Take heed to your selves and to all the flock in which the Holy Spirit has made you guardians, to feed the Church of the Lord which he obtained with his own blood" (Acts 20:28).

Next we come to St. Peter's own idea of his pastoral ministry and that of the bishops of the Church: "So I exhort the elders among you, as a fellow elder and a witness of the sufferings of Christ as well as a partaker in the glory that is to be revealed. Tend the flock of God that is in your charge, not by constraint but willingly, not for shameful gain but eagerly, not as domineering over those in your charge but being examples to the flock. And when the chief Shepherd is manifested you will obtain the unfading crown of glory" (1 Pet. 5:1–4).

In this passage we can distinguish three propositions. The first concerns the qualities of the true pastor: these are the very qualities which Jesus had previously commended to the Twelve: disinterestedness, tender care, devotion. They were the qualities which Jesus had particularly impressed on Peter as the one who was to be first among his brethren and the visible foundation of the whole Church; on Peter whose feet he had wished to wash and who had resisted him. Jesus said to him, "What I am doing you do not know now, but afterward you will understand" (John 13:7). If this is interpreted according to the spirit of Jesus and in terms of his own later explanations, it means that at the moment when, through the institution of the Eucharist, he was creating the Church's priesthood, he wanted to make it unmistakably clear that this priesthood was to be principally a service. Peter had evidently understood his Master's will: "Tend the flock of God that is in your charge... not as domineering... but being examples to the flock."

Peter's second proposition is that after Christ's departure a visible pastoral ministry is definitely continued in the Church, charged with a definite mission and consequently invested with a power of spiritual government. Relevant to this point are some words of St. Paul spoken at Miletus to the "elders" of the Church at Ephesus: "Take heed to yourselves and to all the flock, in which the Holy Spirit has made you guardians, to feed the Church of the Lord, which he obtained with his own blood. I know that after my departure fierce wolves will come among you, not sparing the flock" (Acts 20:28–29).

St. Peter finally observes that when on earth men are invested with the pastoral ministry, they are invested as ministers, in essential subordination to him who is *the Prince* of pastors: Jesus who is the *leader* and to whom the flock belongs: "feed *my* lambs, feed *my* sheep" (and cf. John 10:12–13).... The real and the supreme pastor is God, Jesus Christ. We priests have as our charge only the flock *of Jesus;* souls do not belong *to* us, but to him who bought them at a great price. This is a truth that has been proclaimed in solemn joyful tones throughout the tradition of the Church's pastoral ministry. And yet it is a great thing to have the flock and the friends of Jesus in one's care, to have been given the charge of bringing them back to him, or at least of guarding them until he returns and takes them with him so that where he dwells, we may also dwell (John 14:3). And it was also a great thing to have been given the charge of *the whole* flock of Jesus, for our Lord committed all his sheep to him without distinction. There was only one soul in the world that he set apart as, in a sense, exceptional and whose care he committed to the Church in a special way, and that was his mother. She is certainly included in the flock, but since her position in relation to that kingdom to which the pastors must direct the sheep is exceptional, she was committed to the Church for what remained of her life on earth, in a way that was uniquely her own. Jesus, himself, in those hours when he was giving his life for his flock — he who had redeemed Mary beforehand, making her immaculate in her conception — gave her to St. John as his mother (John 19:27)....

According to Eusebius and St. Jerome, Peter the head of the Church was crucified upside down. It seems indeed that his death has a special meaning, for when the Lord, shortly before his ascension, foretold it, he had stressed that he would be "carried," and had added: "Follow me" (John 21:18–19). In Peter's death there is a unique mystery of relationship to Christ which deserves our attention.

Peter is the visible head of the Church, but he is her head as its foundation only because it pleased the Lord to build his Church upon him. Even more accurately, he is her head only as vicar of the real foundation, of him who is the real cornerstone and who has returned forever to the Father's bosom. In this world's buildings the cornerstone is supported by the earth, and gravity, a universal law that holds the world together, causes the stones to adhere to each other, and the whole building to stay firm on the ground. The Church, however, is not a human temple; she is from God and everything in her proceeds from above.... St. John saw her as the new Jerusalem, which unlike the other is not earthly, but comes down from God (Rev. 21:10). Her foundation also is above. While a pilgrim in this world she makes use of human institutions; even so she is not so much built on Peter as suspended from Jesus Christ. It is toward him and through him to the Father that the divine gravitational pull of charity moves; for in the divine world the force of attraction works heavenward and not toward the earth, and it has the torrential power of the living waters of the Spirit with their source in eternal life.

Peter, the visible foundation of the Church and vicar of her true foundation, who has returned to the Father's bosom was crucified upside down, his feet in heaven, invisibly resting on the mystical stone which is Christ. Not only do his feet rest on the invisible foundation; his steps lead the world along the road which is Christ. Together with the keys, he has been entrusted with the ministry of taking us to heaven. The Church, following him, is moving along the new and living road which Christ opened up for us through his blood. The naves of our churches are naves with their keels aloft. They are sailing in heaven.

And this walking upside down in the world, feet aloft, head below, is the only way of obtaining genuine knowledge of the road and of where the journey ends. "If we walk in the light" says St. John (1 John 1:7). Peter is upright in the light. He is, literally, walking in the light. He has the right view of things; it is the world that sees them askew. Peter's head is not really the wrong way up; he is upright in the light, upright at God's side. Peter, head of a Church that, while being in the world, does not originate from the world and may not walk according to the world, leads us heavenward, enables us to walk in the light, even though the worldly-wise consider us fools. For you took possession of the true life and the true wisdom when, accepting the loss of your soul . . . you succeeded in following Jesus to the Father's bosom. "Lord, where are you going?" "Where I am going, you cannot follow me now, but you shall follow me later." "Follow me." —FSL 19–27

ST. THOMAS AQUINAS: SERVANT OF THE TRUTH

In this meditation on Thomas Aquinas as servant of truth, Congar quotes the saint's own sense of his calling: "For my own part, I envisage as the main duty of my life the working out of my debt to God in such a way that I express him in my every word and attitude." Congar interprets this to mean that he intended to be God's servant as a theologian, as a servant of the Truth, and proposes to illustrate "the heroic fulfillment" of his resolve by focusing on Thomas's poverty, purity, and fidelity.

The attitude of a servant is created by poverty. Anyone who is rich, a possessor, ipso facto, cannot be a servant. The possession of external things would intrinsically have little significance if it did not tend to create and develop a definite attitude, an absolute attitude as master and possessor, autonomous and self-sufficient. But the decisive factor in what we are now considering is whether we personally think of ourselves as rich or poor. A man can be a servant only if he is entirely his master's man and instrument, and this he cannot be unless he is poor in spirit, having withdrawn all personal exclusiveness and agreed not to be the master of his own life, retaining nothing as his own and inalienable, and devoting himself wholly to serve: St. Paul exemplifies this when he begins his letters with the words: *Paulus servus Jesu Christi:* "Paul the servant, Jesus Christ's laborer and his man."

Now, when the work in question is God's and particularly when that work consists in speaking about him, then the only possible way of taking part in it is as a servant, that is, primarily as a poor man. Only as a minister and for the work of service is one ever called to it. He who would try to manipulate the things of God as if they were his own — whether in apostolic activity, contemplation, or the grace given for personal spiritual development — refusing to remain poor and trying to become a possessor, immediately loses that personal poverty which is enriched by God and is stripped bare and left to that destitution which, under the deceptive glamour of outward success, is all that remains his own.

It was this attitude of a poor man which Thomas Aquinas, the son of a noble family, the cousin of the Emperor Frederick, more princely in his intellect than in his rank, was to adopt and pursue with the clearest awareness of what God's call demanded from him. He had a profound understanding of the fact that intellectual work, and theological work in particular, depends upon a gift from God; that if we are to serve the truth with loyalty, we need help and light from the Master of minds, and our need is utter. And therefore he, as it were, duplicated his work with prayer. It is a well-known fact that he spent much time in prayer; he prayed before he began working and if some difficulty held him up he turned to God with increased intensity as a beggar. The text of some of these prayers has come down to us. They show that he always approached God as a poor man needing *everything* to be given him, and, on admitting this, did not fear to ask for *everything*....

A further factor is involved. Poverty and the petition of human prayer is the essential condition of all apostolic or even of ordinary Christian activity. But there is a kind of poverty and a form of dependence peculiar to a theologian and concerns his special scientific activity. What, in fact, is theology? It is a human activity that operates upon the datum of the mysteries of faith; it is a work of development, organization, systematization, and of a more thorough understanding of everything that faith can make accessible to the human mind. It is a science, and therefore strictly scientific and rational in its initiatives, methods, and conclusions. And yet it is a science and a rational activity at the root of which lies the whole mystery of the act of faith; a scientific elaboration of data which are not scientific and which exist only for the mind, is in fact only "given," in an act of faith for which reason alone does not suffice. It is a science then, but one that is not content to begin in dependence on its data, which is the common procedure for every discipline; it begins by abdicating the right to verify anything and by receiving its data as children receive the rudiments of knowledge: by faith. Humanly, it is the poorest and most destitute of sciences, and in fact it no longer appears in the official list of sciences.

This was the special kind of service which St. Thomas rendered. He was a servant of God as a theologian. He was poor with the poverty of a servant of God who has nothing of his own; poor as a theologian who does not possess but receives even the principles of his science and who, in the sphere of his special work, may not conduct himself as a master without betraying the law governing his essential position and vocation. When asked for an explanation, the theologian must, sooner or later, drop every view that is merely personal; he must refer to another and point to God. For in the house which he is building he is not the master, but the servant; he is constantly referring to this fact and referring himself to it, for he is only enriched with the wealth of God's wisdom if he accepts the conditions of being himself poor and, in his actual scientific labors, becoming the man and servant of another.

St. Thomas's resolution to be God's servant as a theologian entailed an acceptance of poverty even in the outward organization of his life. Of course, every vocation and all fruitful work implies some renunciation and deprivation; every call to God's service includes in some form the command: "Go from your country and your kindred and your father's house to the land that I will show you" (Gen. 12:1). But we should realize that for St. Thomas this call took on a particular and most definite characteristic. The history and circumstances of his vocation are well known. They are important and very significant as indicating the direction which the young Thomas Aquinas determined his life should take.

Thomas was nineteen when, as a student in Naples, he joined the Friars Preachers. From five to fourteen he had been a Benedictine oblate at Monte Cassino and his family intended that he should have a monastic career in that important abbey, whose territory bordered on that of Aquino, a career that would culminate in his becoming its governor. But what happened? He took the habit of the new order of the Friars Preachers. This means that what he chose, when he had reached adolescence, was not exactly the monastic life, but the life of a Friar Preacher. This was, very definitely, that form of religious life that was devoted to the absolute service of the *Sacra Doctrina*. For this purpose it had renounced the top-heavy alliance with the feudal structure of ecclesiastical organisms as expressed in Monte Cassino, and fairly generally elsewhere. In it the spiritual power and its ministry had become heavily bogged down in the temporal order. The consequences of his decision are famous. When his family received the news that he had joined the Dominicans and also had immediately left for north Italy and France, they decided to capture the young novice, and did so. Thomas was waylaid, seized, confined in isolation, and subjected to pressure — of an infamous kind — to make him give up the Dominican habit. But, as the documents show, what they wanted him to give up was not the monastic but the Dominican life, and that to which he held was not simply the monastic life — this was not under dispute — it was also and no less strongly, the Dominican life, the monastic life in its Dominican form.

Clearly, the young Thomas Aquinas had made a choice based on the soundest reflection, and with lucid determination. And it all points in one direction. At nineteen, as surely as in later life, he would not commit himself to anything secondary; this is all the more evident from the fact that throughout his career we can observe a definite series of such determined choices. What is the significance of this?

All the documentary evidence, as well as the historical circumstances relating to the idea behind the origin of the Friars Preachers (and in addition what St. Thomas himself was later to express in one of those limpid phrases that leave nothing further to be said), shows that the order made its appeal to his youthful enthusiasm, as the order that was at the service of the truth. Of course all the orders serve the truth, but this one made the very reason for its existence the creation of a way of serving God through that work of charity which consists in contemplating the truth and communicating it. It was a religious life, adaptable without opportunism, broadminded without false liberalism, passionate in defense of the faith without partisanship, amazingly adapted to a life that stemmed from the truth and for the truth, from the Word of God and for it, in which intellectual activity, applied to God himself, became the reality which was sanctified and offered to God as an act of worship.

Thomas chose the Preachers and clung to the scapular of St. Dominic because it was the order at the service of the truth, the order in which detachment from the world was best organized to serve the truth. He was later offered high ecclesiastical positions; in particular, after his family had been ruined as the result of its fidelity to the pope, he was offered, as a means to its assistance, the archbishopric of Naples or the abbacy of Monte Cassino. But even though his concern for his family stands out in a number of ways, he firmly refused and prayed for the grace not to change from the path he had chosen. And to avoid all deception as to the real significance and implication of such a prayer, it is to be observed that St. Thomas asked God through the intercession of the Blessed Virgin Mary, not only that he personally should be preserved in his calling as a Friar Preacher, but also that the nature of the order should never be changed. Finally, at the end of his life, when he had left Naples and was on that unfulfilled last journey to the Council of Lyons and already gravely ill, his companion and friend Reginald expressed sorrow, for he had hoped, he said, that the pope would reward the services of Brother Thomas Aquinas (as he had those of St. Bonaventure) by making him a cardinal. Thomas replied, "Have no regrets about that, for among the petitions I have made to God—and I thank him that they have been heard—is a request that I may be taken from this world in the same humble state of life in which I now am, and that I may be given no dignity or office that would change it."

Similar quotations could he multiplied. One thing at any rate is certain: in the case of a man as fully conscious of what he did and of what he wanted as was Thomas Aquinas, such a prayer is packed with meaning. It signified that for him the order of St. Dominic represented a state of poverty in the broadest and most positive sense, organized in a form of religious life: a state in which religious poverty not only produced freedom from temporal cares, but through an added spiritual refinement also produced freedom, even in the domain of the apostolate itself, from all the practical affairs of government and administration which still form a kind of island of the temporal within the spiritual. The poverty required for the service of the truth by one who is God's contemplative and theologian extends, in St. Thomas's view, to this renunciation and abandonment of everything to do with offices in the practical and administrative order. This, of course, throws no discredit on such offices and in no way denies that men may be faithful to the service of God and to contemplation, in the field of action or government. But we have to admit that, in his view, both his personal vocation and that of his order as a corporate body at the service of the truth, implies such absolute deprivation, such utter willingness to serve, a poverty so total that he, personally, and his order also, must remain in the condition of a simple servant of the unblemished truth, in the condition of the simplicity of life of a theologian.

Purity is the positive aspect of this poverty understood as a broad and deep attitude of the soul. Like poverty, this attitude makes service possible and gives one the disposition to be a servant; as purity, it is the total, integral, and, so to say, virginal characteristic of service. A pure man is one who is not tainted, not a mixture of vice and virtue, not morally defective or contaminated, not reduced in stature, but integral, uncorrupted, whole, and absolute. Poverty is therefore that which enables the unadulterated nature of purity to exist. St. Thomas was a pure servant, a virginal and chaste servant because he was first of all personally poor, wholly the man of him whom he called Lord.

The service of the angelic doctor was regally pure. To start with he had that bodily chastity which we usually identify with purity though often not realizing why the Christian mind attaches such importance to it. If we are to appreciate its worth we should perhaps envisage it not only in itself but in what it makes possible, or what its opposite prevents. In reality, purity understood in the narrow and ordinary sense as chastity of body, imagination, and desire, involves the whole spiritual life, because it opens — and its opposite closes — every possible relationship with God. Consider a soul that is crude and impure: it will not deny the teachings of the faith, but it becomes hardened and ends by shutting itself off from the finest elements of that faith; its spiritual sensitivity dulls; it will not reject the central dogmas, but their noblest content no longer interests it: the Virgin, the angels, the sacraments, the religious life, contemplation; it comes to assert that nothing can be known about them and that they do not exist. A pure soul, on the contrary, instinctively opens itself out to these things; it experiences them to the extent in which it is sensitively pure. It would seem that faithfulness on this point opens its eyes and provides the evidence which crudity would instantaneously conceal. It realizes with certainty that its development is an immediate relationship with the sensitivity and fidelity of its life.

We can now have a somewhat clearer idea of what purity, bodily purity, meant for St. Thomas in the work of service as a theologian to which he was called, and we can see to what extent it was a positive element in his soul as a servant of the truth. We need hardly stress here the famous scene of his temptation — it has been in any case a little touched up — or the testimony given after his death by his most intimate friend that he had always preserved the purity of a child.

There is, however, a deeper aspect of his purity as a servant of the truth; it is that of the inner purity of his soul, in the most positive and fullest sense of that word. As a correlative to poverty considered as a fundamental attitude of the soul, this purity of the servant of the truth consists in allowing no admixture of self to enter into this truth, no toning down, no rejection, but instead a complete self-surrender to its demands and an acceptance of the Other, the Master, as he really is in himself and not as we might have imagined him to be. It is he, the Master, who must be in control, he who must be affirmed in the truth of his own nature, and allowed to do what he wills, whereas I, his servant, affirm nothing of myself apart from him, but am totally at his service, entirely subject to him, wholly his "minister."

This purity of a servant shines out in the life of St. Thomas. It shines out in his prayers in which every phrase expresses his anxiety to give punctilious service and not to botch God's work by any of the many imperfections, the pettiness, the off-handedness, the self-indulgence in which even the best intentions are squandered. "Make me, my Lord and God, obedient without contradiction, poor without wavering, chaste without corruption, patient without protest, humble without pretence, joyful without becoming dissipated, sad without being wretched, grave but not unbending, active but not frivolous, living in thy fear without discouragement, sincere without affectation, doing good without presumption, correcting other's without pride, building them up in word and deed without dishonesty." And there are many similar prayers. We should not be deceived by the concern shown for stylistic precision in them; what St. Thomas is trying to express is not a faultless statement of moral theology, but the ideal of faultless service, service that reaches perfection and the utmost sensitivity, service that shall not in anyway botch God's work.

This purity of his service shines out also in its integral, unrestricted, unadulterated character. He was utterly a servant, waiting at his master's door with all available strength and every means at his disposal. In his life there was no division, not one part for his own purposes and another for God's service: he was utterly a servant, integrally serving. In himself, he was completely poor, and that this might be, he was, without qualification, the servant of the Other, of his Master. On our part we often fail in this, sometimes deliberately, because we prefer to control and enjoy things for our own sake, rather than put ourselves at God's disposal; more often we fail through weakness and forgetfulness, because we are seldom wholly engaged in what we are doing and therefore our effective service mobilizes only a half or a third of our personality. Service that is total and wholly unqualified can be given only by great souls (and this is true of an absolute refusal to serve: Nietzsche). If we remember that, according to St. Thomas, the need — resulting from a perfect insight into reality — of turning to God and of moving toward him with all our strength or of turning away from him completely and forever, is a privilege of the angels, we shall realize one of the soundest reasons why his integral and pure service has earned him the magnificent title of the "angelic doctor."

Lastly, the purity of his service of the truth shines out from the fact that he scrupulously refrained from intruding himself into what he had decided to serve, from adding or subtracting anything from the truth he served. In this service he was pure by aiming to become, as far as possible, a pure instrument. In his theological activity he was a "minister" in the fullest meaning of the word; his teaching career was that of a priest. In his *Summa* alone, he wrote more than three thousand articles, and in none of them, except here and there when he wished to retract some statement, does he speak of himself; there is not one of them that is not like a monstrance behind which the theologian hides in order to exhibit his God. It is an unprecedented example of purity, of priestly detachment and virginity. This man certainly left his homeland and his relations. Apart from the truth, apart from the subject dealt with, it is difficult to know with whom we are in relationship. Is it a prince, a Frenchman, someone old, a partisan of the emperor, an Italian noble? It is not evident; but he is a priest, he exhibits his God and conceals himself; he is a theologian, a minister of the Word, a minister of the objective truth; as a person he is hidden. This is very moving; in fact nothing is more moving than this kind of impersonality in his teaching. It shows none of the characteristics of an individual nor displays his temperament. Hence its seeming lack of tragic conflict; no human sounds are audible, and only the radiation of objective reality is apparent. The "Behold the handmaid of the Lord, be it done to me according to your word" has once again been spoken and lived: I am only a servant; be it done according to your word.

We can now see that this purity, the positive aspect of an attitude of personal poverty in a genuine servant, brings about the special virtue and perfection of a servant's soul: fidelity.... Fidelity is a servant's special virtue because it is a virtue of attachment to another, and a servant, as such, does the work of another, exists for another. Only if he is faithful can he truly serve and he will be faithful if he fulfils the expectation and the trust bestowed upon him. This involves two main qualities: constancy and probity — two qualities eminently present in St. Thomas. His fidelity as a servant displayed itself principally as constancy in his external life and as probity in his inmost soul.

His service was no outward show or gilded idleness. The fullness of his life and the intensity of his work are almost incredible. He died at forty-nine, leaving a life's work which fills thirty large quarto volumes in which there is no slip in the process of his thought or in his reasoning. If we read his biography or the depositions made during the preparations for his canonization (depositions which in other cases are sometimes lacking in real content), we observe that all the witnesses emphasize the impressive way in which every day of his life formed an unbroken continuity of work and prayer.... All these depositions are unanimous in reporting, together with the testimony on his purity, this characteristic which seems to have left an abiding impression: he was a man who did not give a minute of his life to any other thing than the immediate service of the truth through the contemplation and teaching of doctrine. It is manifest that when he became aware of his vocation as a theologian he not only allowed himself no further waste of time but also would have nothing to do with anything that he considered would prove to be a distraction from his wholehearted service of the truth and from his consecration to it. He carried out to the letter his words in the *Contra Gentiles:* "For my own part, I envisage as the main duty of my life the working out of my debt to God in such a way that I express him in my every word and attitude." This was his personal asceticism, his fidelity as a servant. He let none of the little things with which his Lord had entrusted him be pushed aside. "Because you have been faithful in little things: we shall soon discover his reward."

And yet what is perhaps most moving in his fidelity as the servant of truth is his soul's infinite sensitivity and immense respect for that truth, to which he owed and gave loyal service, and which was his master's property and not his own. Fidelity in the sense of probity, integrity, disinterestedness, is, in fact, the special and decisive virtue of a servant. It presupposes an attitude of both poverty and purity and is its consummation. Through this St. Thomas achieved his perfect service.

His utmost respect was given to the whole data of revelation and extended to its furthest reaches, for he had received it as a deposit from God. He held the stewardship of property that was his master's, not his own, and what is expected of a steward and a servant is that he should be faithful. Hence it is that we can observe in St. Thomas that extraordinary sensitivity in avoiding the least betrayal of the truth, in not exaggerating and not minimizing what had been given, or rather, committed to him, that extraordinary prudence in thought, assertion, and mode of expression. His work and teaching, as is well known, are characterized by its establishment of an equilibrium of every point of view; it has a breadth and power that can incorporate and coordinate all things. This does not mean that he was not one of those who, having a deeper penetration than others, are more conscious of the differences between things; but he also belonged to those who, from a higher altitude, can see what is universal and multiple in an idea; and, most importantly, he belonged to those servants who have a reverential care to lose nothing and to bring out the true worth of all the things which their master has confided to them. He was an eminently Catholic genius, because he served the very principle of Catholicity.

As a result of this he could combine a most acute appreciation of God's absolute preeminence and of the total primacy of his initiative in the soul's activity, with a steady and sensitive respect for the different natures in the created world and for the laws that govern them. For this reason also he was able to unite at the highest level the sense of the reasonableness of the faith and of its mystery. He did not believe that everything could be demonstrated, or penetrated by the mind, but neither did he underestimate the activity of the believing mind in contemplating and working out the implications of the revealed data.... He was only a servant, but he would not be forced to say that a theologian's contribution is nothing.

He also held together in unity the validity of the speculative intelligence and its rational conclusions, the absolute value of a metaphysical knowledge, the inescapable reality of a fact, the importance of a critical control of documentary sources. In his theological work he incorporated with equal reverence the Eastern testimonies of the Christian tradition with those of the West. Throughout his work he combines an unparalleled sense of the unity of things and the wisdom corresponding to this unity, with the strictest methodological requirements, a scrupulous honesty with regard to the object under consideration and the special treatment it demands. When this is lacking, he says, believers tend to affirm that something has been demonstrated when in fact it has not, and thus provoke the mockery of unbelievers at themselves, and what is more important, at the *faith*. And this danger deeply disturbed his loyal sense of service.

Thanks to his blameless service St. Thomas did not exclude the least ray, the least speck of the sun. Not a single aspiration of the soul was dealt with lightly or superficially by him, or treated harshly or brushed aside. No one in contact with this dialectical giant would be made to lose his simplicity of mind and heart; he himself, on a level with the sages of the world, confronted the Gospel with the simplicity of St. Francis of Assisi.

Moreover, it is because he was in this way a faithful servant that he truly is the "common doctor." ... Certainly he is the common teacher, the man who belongs to all men, because he does not belong to himself, but to the truth, to which all have a right and to which all men belong. This is why he is universally trusted; no one is afraid that he will snatch anything that is theirs, that he will want to grab something for himself. Everyone knows that he will give only one thing: truth.

It is to this absolute faithfulness as a servant that he owed the courage and the spirit of adventure that is expressed in his work. This servant, this supporter of continuity, this traditionalist, this disciple of all previous thinkers, is also astoundingly venturesome. He takes up Aristotle, whom the hierarchy still suspect; he writes an apparently simple phrase — and it proves to have explosive consequences; he lays down principles whose conclusions and infective power have not yet reached their consummation.

In reality he was bold because he was simple and courageous, because he was a servant. A man who does not work for his own ends, but in the service of someone greater than himself, far from being enslaved is delivered from everything beneath him. Nothing braver can be found than a young heart, not loaded with wealth, but pure and faithful, with nothing to fear and nothing to lose. A servant of this kind is endowed with pride, certainty and audacity. But it is a pride coupled with personal humility, a certainty that is wholly mistrustful of self, an audacity that knows its own limitations. It has no personal fear, nothing personal to lose, but he is in charge of a treasure for which everything else may be abandoned.

Such a man was St. Thomas. His life has a profound message for us. We must be authentic servants in order that we may become free and independent of everything which, in our master's service, should be employed only as a means and an instrument. We must be authentic servants in order that we may become prudent and able to avoid even the slightest misuse of that which does not belong to us.

To bring this consideration of St. Thomas as a servant of the truth to a close, we should penetrate even deeper and uncover the true and living root of this service. Its quality is such that it can have been achieved only through love and in a mutual relationship of love. A bodily submission to another person is possible from fear and necessity, and without love. But it is impossible, without love, to submit one's soul to another person, or to give oneself in spiritual service. Unadulterated service is incompatible with lovelessness. For such service implies working for another without keeping back anything for oneself, and that means that the other's interests have been made one's own, and no wish, no pleasure is indulged apart from those of the master. It is such an absolute donation, uncontaminated with self, that in fact the other's life becomes one's own, more real than the self itself. Only love can do this, for only love produces ecstasy, the exodus from self, only love can allow a master, the mastery of one's soul.

The source, therefore, of that perfect service of the truth to which St. Thomas devoted his life, was this warm, personal, and vital relationship with the truth which we call love, or in Christian terminology, charity. This was due to the fact that, for him, the truth was not merely an object of knowledge, not merely an idea, not even a thing, but a living person to be loved, a living and merciful person who begins by offering himself to our love and by inserting in our frozen souls the warm and vital seed of friendship. This "truth" is, in reality, "the gentle primal truth," the living God of Abraham, Isaac, and Jacob, the adorable Trinity, the Savior-God, indeed the incarnate Word, the truth who is Jesus Christ....

When St. Thomas was dying at Fossanova, "he wanted to receive our Lord's body, and when it was brought to him, he knelt down and hailed and adored it, saying at length these wonderful words, 'I receive thee, the price of my soul's redemption, I receive thee, Viaticum, the journey money of my pilgrimage, for whose love I have studied, watched, labored, preached, and taught. . . .' " Thus he tells us the secret of that lifelong service, at the beginning of which he had said, "For my own part, I envisage as the main duty of my life the working out of my debt to God in such a way that I express him in my every word and attitude." That secret, the motive of his life, was love. . . . He did not carry out this overwhelming work of service, those thirty years of incredible labor without a moment's infidelity, for any other reason than his love of this most hidden friend, for this sacrament before which we have fewer resources than for any other reality, because our conviction of its truth depends upon faith alone. And when the dying saint, who had never spoken an idle word, explained the reason for all that he had done, it was that he had loved.

Finally, a witness records that one evening during the last months of St. Thomas's life, he followed him in order to observe him. He came into the back of the chapel of St. Nicholas where St. Thomas was deep in prayer. He then saw that he had been raised from the ground. . . . Suddenly, from the direction toward which our master had turned, a voice from the crucifix was heard: "Thomas, you have written well of me; what reward would you receive from me for your labors?" He answered, "Lord, nothing but thyself." These words are the last words; the service of the truth, of God, has been consummated. Thomas had been a faithful servant; he had written well, worked well. What was his reward to be? The good servant's reward, the servant who has been unreservedly true and served from love alone, is his master's intimate friendship, the sharing of his joy. For the only reward of love is love, and if a man will remain poor and chaste and faithful in his service, because he is the Bridegroom's friend (John 3:24), then his reward will be the Bridegroom's joy. —FSL 68–83

Congar's little essays on the saints are good examples of the countless occasional pieces he wrote throughout his life, even at his busiest, for a number of French journals and newspapers. His bibliography, after all, stretches to well over two thousand items! In addition, he also wrote theological pieces in a more popular vein, almost sermons, and other essays that would probably be classed as "spirituality." Extracts from several of these pieces follow here.

CHRISTMAS IS, FIRST OF ALL, JESUS CHRIST

We are witnessing a kind of secularization of Christmas. Christmas, it is said, is the children's feast, the feast of family intimacy. Who, on that day, fails to feel kindness stirring in his heart, the wish to be good, to bring comfort to the ailing or to those in trouble, to make some gesture of peace and friendship? Even in war a kind of truce is arranged on that day; it would be shameful to kill and natural to offer the enemy a drink.

There is the Christmas tree, and lights, and presents. And yet, in those illuminated cities, Christmas is tending to become the conclusion and pretext for a huge commercial season that begins in the early days of December. Advent is becoming a season of commercial advertising. Recently in a room full of soldiers, one of them, a Mohammedan, was celebrating Moulin, that is the Birth of the Prophet. A conscript seminarian took the opportunity of saying, "We too celebrate the birth of our God as savior of mankind." He was startled to realize that many of his comrades simply did not know that Christmas was just that.

Goodness itself has its dangers. For instance, it is becoming increasingly common for Christian families on that day to welcome to their table those who have no home of their own. They call to mind that once there was a mother and her young husband, the birth of whose child was at hand; they were told that there was no lodging available for them. They had no friends and the only welcome awaiting them was among the animals in a cave used as a stable.

We have heard this theme developed in sermons to the effect that for the proper observance of Christmas we should invite a refugee, a colored student, a poor man, to spend it with us. Of course there is truth in this, and yet Christmas is first of all Jesus Christ. A friendly gesture of this kind only becomes truly Christian when faith's teaching about this day has been accepted as true. Once that has been done light and warmth can radiate unchecked.

Confronted by these dangers and in view of the secularization in progress Christians have been neither inert nor passive. The title of this article was itself taken from a poster, pasted on the walls or displayed in shop windows in Strasbourg, as a result of a Catholic and Protestant initiative approved by the authorities of each. This fact suggests one of the main reasons for our joy as Christians: Christmas is an ecumenical feast. For us Christians, who are at present divided, Christmas is something common to us all, not only as regards the calendar or the social customs connected with it but because we agree on the essential meaning of the festival: Christmas is Jesus Christ, first of all: Jesus Christ who "is always the same yesterday, today, and for ever" (Heb. 13:8)....

How great our need that he should come! He came once in the humility of the flesh: he will come back one day in the power of his glory. He comes each day, spiritually, through the ministry of the Church, through the priests and the laity who are his witnesses. For us Frenchmen, our fair France has at this time become France in distress, a France at war in Algeria, and therefore in mourning. The whole world is a world in distress, for it too is everywhere at war whether the war be hot or cold. Such are the conditions in which this year we must say, and say courageously, with the energy and the accent of truth: Glory be to God on high, and on earth peace to men of good will (Luke 2:14).

What does that mean for us? It means something which at first sight seems too sublime, too spiritual to be applicable to our human situation, and yet which is the absolute and decisive truth about that condition. This is the truth which the Church offers in the Gospel of a votive Mass which I, personally, have often celebrated: the votive Mass for peace. This Gospel is taken from St. John (20:19–23). Again it is not peace in general, the peace which men arrange and violate; it is the peace of Jesus Christ. It is inseparable from that forgiveness of sins of which the astounding ministry was entrusted to the apostles. In short, its profound source is the radiation of God's love upon us, within us, and through us upon other men, just as the profound source of war is sin. It is often said that if there was a good God there would be no war. But would it not be truer to say that if we obeyed God, if we put the Gospel into practice, there would be no war? Christmas can, once again, become the origin of that peace which we desire, or rather, which mankind *absolutely needs.*

On one condition: that it is authentic, not a mere word, not a ceremony, not folklore. In short, on condition that it is Jesus Christ coming in his real personality into our hearts as into a living crib. And this time may he be listened to and obeyed with absolute sincerity. —RG 63–66

THE THREE AGES OF THE SPIRITUAL LIFE

In this article I intend to analyze the essential conditions for an adult spiritual life, with a special reference to the experience of men. We shall take three elements that seem to provide the needed characteristics for defining the respective stages of childhood, adolescence, and manhood: adolescence has the appearance of a special intermediary period containing some of the features of childhood and foreshadowing those of manhood without yet possessing them. The third element will provide an opportunity for some discussion of what may be called (for the men) the crisis at forty-five. These will be simply notes intended to provoke thought, and I realize that they are exceedingly schematic. In spite of this, however, I trust that they will prove useful.

I

A child is wrapped up in his body and his appetites, themselves determined by the needs of his body. He is also wholly self-centered, egocentric even in his affections. His charm and naïveté, the instinctive tendency of his elders to flatter his weakness, prevent this egocentric characteristic from becoming offensive. And yet a child is, in fact, entirely focused upon getting what he wants, and his wants are themselves controlled by his physical needs.

The adolescent discovers his strength. He is entering for some years into a condition in which the organism, in possession of its stature, strength, and generative power, gains more than it loses. Hence his zest for expanded interests and enterprise. This is the age of varied ambitions (not yet for a single ambition, which tends to be miserly and crudely realistic). But this zest for expansion and enterprise does not necessarily imply self-giving: it may remain simply a desire for self-fulfillment. The adolescent is controlled by the desire to fulfill himself, and he gladly welcomes everything which he considers can help him to develop, to increase his strength, to bring his life to perfection.

The adult lives for others; he is a source of life to others. This is due to a de facto situation and not to a kind of sublime or heroic devotion: the adult normally has a family and a profession. Through the latter he becomes a producer, and this gives him a responsibility for the lives of others. From every point of view he is as it were physically compelled to live with others in mind, and to give himself. Self-giving is written into his situation; it is less poetic, but far more real than that of the adolescent.

There is of course a further transition to be made; it is the transition from the adult condition, which is simply the outcome of life itself and of the instincts that accompany life, to a religion, a faith, a grown-up spiritual life. Spiritually, a man is not truly adult unless in his soul he passes from an attitude which is egocentric or expansive for his own ends, to a self-possession and control of his resources with the aim of self-giving. This is obviously an ideal. Many men have grown-up bodies and occupy an adult position in the world, and yet their souls have not grown up. A man is spiritually adult only if his life's activities are determined by his spirit and not by bodily or extrinsic impulses; only if he has integrated his various inclinations within the unity of the self, with a spiritual life-principle, with an ultimate goal. In Christian theology, this corresponds to the program of theological humanism of the kind envisaged by Thomist ethics, governed by charity, the virtue of the end, and by prudence, the virtue of the means. It also corresponds to the program of the royal priesthood or of spiritual kingship which consists of self-offering and self-giving and, in order to attain this, the achievement, self-possession, and self-control, becoming the true ruler in one's own kingdom, so that the attempt to master one's passions is an affair for children; their education should demand it from them. But adults, they hold, are dispensed from carrying it on and, exhausted by the tension produced by their work, give up the effort to control themselves in any other sphere than work. Religion could be of great assistance in this matter, provided that it is presented to them as something real and demanding.

Since an adult has acquired self-possession he is able to do wholly what a child or an adolescent can do only partially, because self-possession has not yet been acquired. An adult is (ought to be) a person in his own right; he is not only that which his body, his parents, his environment have made of him; he is himself the creative subject of relationships to which he can give their truth. He is, he can be, fully responsible, someone who may be appealed to and counted on. He can hold his own in his environment, in the work to be done, even in the development of history, of the world and the Church. With his experience of that which has lasting value, of that which is really worthwhile, he is able to maintain an unpretentious position maturely. With a realist's grasp of life and of his own place in the world, he is able to take his part in work of long duration, to avoid impatience, and to endure.

The major element in the formation of an adult Christian life will consist of the discovering of one's exact position in the world and in the Church, a discovery to be followed by corresponding commitments. Not necessarily sublime, ambitious, and global commitments, and yet real commitments, resulting from tried convictions, from an accurate knowledge of ourselves, of the state of the world and of the Church, according to our abilities to understand them. It should be realized that Catholic Action has been for very many men and women a most practical means of adult education by enabling them to discern the dimensions of the world and where precisely we are committed to the service of God and men. And yet we still need books with the power to awaken and sustain a genuine spiritual life. The lives of the saints and many works on spirituality are, even today, stamped with an unhealthy romanticism, by a systematic overstatement and adulation, sometimes by a triviality that has no relationship with adult behavior, but at most—and this is still a feature of them—with that exuberant enthusiasm of children which is generous, but somewhat unreal. From a theological point of view this indicates the lack of a sound doctrine of man and a latent monophysitism, that is, the real conditions of human nature are dodged. I most earnestly hope that lives of the saints and works of spirituality will be written that will show how holiness is attained through simple but real decisions and deeds that are the outcome of a genuinely human life. The immense success and fruitfulness of the Counter-Reformation in the sixteenth century was largely due to the realism of the men who opened schools, taught the catechism, looked after the sick, founded pious associations, or gave retreats with a definite moral and spiritual program adapted to the needs of the times.

II

A child lives its life in dependence upon another. A man's life history is that of the stages, beginning in his mother's womb, by which he becomes established in the world. At first he lives literally in and from his mother.

After he has physically departed from her womb, she is still for several years his source of life; he looks to her for protection, and turns to his parents for everything, and relies on them. From them he receives the directives for his life. Since they normally are only interested in his welfare and look after him affectionately because of his frailty, he trusts them. Faith is easy at his age and he lives by faith. The answers given to his questions satisfy him and he is reassured. I shall comment later on the deep-seated relationship between this attitude of trust and faith and the religious attitude. When our Lord said that the kingdom of heaven belongs to children and to those who remember them, it was this attitude he had in mind. St. Paul, on the other hand, said: "Do not be children in your thinking; be babes in evil, but in thinking be mature" (1 Cor. 14–20).

The discovery of his own strength, which is the mark of the adolescent, makes him discard the search for props and cease to live with reference to others and by proxy, which is the typical feature of childhood. Since he gains his strength only by separating himself from that attitude of dependence and constant reference, he reacts against his family circle, and in general against all authority that attempts to impose its will upon him, unless he considers that he can make use of it for the purposes of this self-fulfillment, which is his main concern. And yet in spite of this elemental need for nonconformity, he still has few ideas that are genuinely his own; his outlook depends not on personal experience, for as yet he has had none, but on the various trends of thought around him (for example, Marxism, existentialism, surrealism, and also on such things as scouting and technical interests of a mechanical kind). It is the age of gangs and camping, when ideologies win fervent adherents, an age of frank iconoclasm, and also an age that is easily deceived.

An adult assumes (ought to assume) responsibility for his life. This happens in the nature of things; he has a profession, a home of his own, and no one stands by to tell him what he should do. He does it by instinct, and he will not easily tolerate the dictates of others with regard to how he should behave.

In his *Mission of St. Benedict* Newman remarks that a child lives principally by his imagination, an adult by logic and reasoning, and a mature man by experience. An adolescent depends much on the ideas around him and on the social atmosphere, but an adult becomes more personal, acquires his own convictions from his contacts with facts and experience. To a degree that varies with this character, culture, and *Sitz im Leben,* he escapes from the ready-made ideas of his environment and gains a clearer view of things as they really are. This is why, although still holding his own as a man and not being afraid to arrive at a position in opposition to others as a result of decisions he has taken, he becomes, as a rule, more tolerant and esteems and respects every genuine achievement. He has a better idea of the difficulty, the cost, and the real worth of things.

These qualities, sound enough in themselves, may entail serious religious difficulties. He has taken his life's conduct into his own hands, and he may become obsessed by a sense of demiurgic power and self-creating sufficiency. Men who have succeeded and won for themselves a position in life will find it difficult to retain that sense of dependence and childlikeness that is the essence of a religious soul. *A fortiori,* they find it impossible to believe in the somewhat naive presentation of religious matters which unfortunately is all too frequent. Good enough, they say, for women and children, and, apart from the respect due to these latter, we are often bound to agree with them. There are ways of speaking about the sacraments, the Blessed Virgin, St. Joseph, which deserve this judgment. They condemn us. St. Thomas Aquinas, for instance, took a very dim view of expositions of the faith which provoked or justified the *irrisio infidelium,* the scoffing of unbelievers.

Here we approach a point of great importance with respect to the adult quality of belief and especially its virility. The development of a life consists in authenticating in oneself, critically, a number of choices made or accepted in a general way at its start: the choice of a profession, of a wife and children; or those not chosen, but accepted and ratified: that of one's country, language, and culture, and, above all, for a Christian, that of faith; for a priest and a monk that of his priesthood and monastic life.

In one sense a man never gives himself more fully to all this, is never more united with it, than in the beginning. When things begin they have an intensity and a genuineness that is perhaps never surpassed. Péguy has expressed this thought in words that have the freshness and depth of a spring of living water. Bergson[3] may have inspired them (the life-force: self-formation in contrast to the ready-made), but they express, nevertheless, a fundamental truth. In a sense we have never been closer to Christ than on the day of our first communion, on the evening of our ordination or of our religious profession; never more truly at one in our marriage than on our wedding day. And yet how much more real our priesthood is after twenty years of dutiful service, how much more thoroughly religious, more intimately bound to God and his interests twenty-five years after our religious profession than in the fervor of the novitiate; how much deeper twenty-five years of conjugal fidelity, with its mutual support, its trials, its mutual sharing of joys and difficulties, has made the relationship between the partners.

How much deeper is the ratification we bestow in maturity upon some choice we made in our youth. Life may have erased much of its poetry, but it has made certain of its soundness. My life as a priest, a monk, a man of faith, a married and family

3. Henri Bergson (1859–1941), a major French philosopher, author of *Creative Evolution* and the concept of the *élan vital.*

man, an adult and mature citizen of my country, has been purified by trials and strengthened by fidelity and thus the principles of my early choice have been confirmed through the testing-time of difficulties and obstacles. The qualities of adult belief presuppose a similar purification.

But this meets great dangers. When we criticize our beliefs, as well as our choices and commitments, in order to make sure that they are authentic, there is a risk that the corrosive acid of criticism may dissolve them. It frequently happens that the effects of disillusionment and ill will, of the critical spirit and often bitter experience attack not only the spontaneity, but the very essence of what was originally given, and it is retracted bit by bit, even though the outward façade is kept up from habit. There are others, of course, who neither question nor criticize anything, but the danger with this is that they may never cross over from appearance to reality, from the social to the personal, from childishness to manhood. These are two grave distortions which a really adult development should avoid or overcome.

It has never been easy to become a man, either in the realm of faith, or of the emotions, or of culture. It is a comparatively easy matter to diagnose the trouble, at least in its main lines. Its treatment and therapy are not so simple. At any rate much is gained by knowing what should be done.

A child cannot distinguish between what is imaginary and what is real. For him the invisible is as real as the visible, and the two are in continuity. All of us remember having seen, actually seen, the hooded man roaming in the night, the furred creature at the bottom of the garden, the little bird coming out of the camera. At first a child has no idea of the exact limits of an object, of its coherence, and still less of its degree of permanence. That is why his testimony, even when subjectively sincere, is of little worth. Since he cannot define the boundary between what he imagines and what in fact he sees, he cannot be held responsible for an account of objective truth, and his certainty has little foundation. But it is precisely this fact that makes him alive to symbols. For him, little Jesus really is inside the tabernacle; he sees him at the elevation; he knows that his mother can read, inscribed on his forehead, any untruth he may tell.

There is, moreover, a natural and untroubled harmony between his mental outlook and the religious attitude; that attitude is, as we have seen, sustained by faith from start to finish and trusts instinctively. We now see that it also connects symbol with reality; the reality of sacred history, the sacraments, the invocation and presence of the Invisible — all this is easily accepted. The kingdom of heaven does indeed belong to those who share these characteristics. But how dangerous it would be if religion remained at the stage of childhood and if it never advanced beyond a magical idea of God and the sacraments. How desirable it is to acquire the judgment of grown men, and how great is the responsibility of priests like myself to train our people to become adults in religion.

Adolescence is the age when reason takes up its place in mental activity, creative work, and practical pursuits. This is an event that occurs at an early date, at the threshold of rational life, in that period we call the age of reason. A little later, it develops into an intense desire to know where we stand, to escape being deceived by appearances or erroneous explanations. The outline of the realities that throng the world is becoming definite. And yet adolescence has not really reached this goal. It is still the age of broad general vision, of endless discussions on the widest issues, of unbounded ambition where there seems to be no barrier to what is possible; it is the age of poetry, of unselfish illusions. In a sense it is an age of happiness. Only in youth, says popular wisdom, does one yield to folly. But such folly is very often an introduction to the future; youth may not yet be learned, but old age may be impotent. Mgr. Gibier[4] has remarked: "illusions are like leaves; through them we breathe."

4. Charles Henri Gibier (1849–1931), French priest and bishop of Versailles from 1906 to 1931.

When a man has grown up he gains a vivid awareness of the world's reality, of the boundary lines of its constituent elements, their inflexibility and their power to endure. In fact, it is the experience of this power to endure that enables them to be clearly defined. The result is realism, and with it often bitter disillusionment. We have now reached a point of great importance: the crisis of middle age or of forty-five years. It is less revolutionary than that of adolescence, but it is equally profound and perhaps less difficult to overcome. It does not offer an entry into a new world of exciting possibilities, but rather an extinction of such possibilities. The problem becomes a matter not of fresh discovery but of what is worthwhile retaining.

We shall try to confront these issues in a way that an adult can accept.

The crisis affects our calling and also the certainty of the decisions and principles on which we have staked our life. For we learn from experience, and when we realize that we have reached the point at which life is beginning to decline, and that now our achievements will not be appreciably better than they have been in the past, or even different from them, we take stock of our position with some sadness. An officer in the army realizes that the end of his command is in sight; the business man is conscious that an error committed early in his career will always prove frustrating. The heights we hoped to climb are beyond us forever. The promising children we cherished have failed us; the more we have hoped from them, the more we have loved them, the greater our suffering. We add up our failures and the opposition we have encountered and we see that we cannot be fooled about the future. Even a man who has been materially successful may have met disaster in his affections; and although he may have put honesty and his family's name above the chances of material gain, he knows now that it is not true that the good are rewarded and the wicked punished.

A gloomy sense of frustration drives a man to seek some compensation. This is the hour of the noonday devil, of *ersatz* success or consolation, or even of some minimal satisfaction.

Between the successful catch or the horserace won odds-on, a petty kingship achieved, how many niches, how many brands of alibi exist for the man deceived? Some, of course, do not yield an inch; they courageously entrench themselves, but in their souls an element of sterile bitterness and of more or less vivid disillusionment remains.

A new situation needs to be created. As with many moral problems the initial effort must be made by the mind. This is too often forgotten, and moral and voluntary effort is wasted because we have not first corrected our ideas. Very often in difficulties which, for example, we experience with a neighbor, the best intentions, the most sincere resolves, come to grief, because between them and the concrete act false ideas intervene that have never been seriously corrected. The first thing to do is to assess the situation, to accept it and meet it realistically. We need to reinterpret our position in the world as it really is, and then to be willing to accept it when we find, as we probably shall, that it is a modest one. Our misfortunes and failings are largely due to the fact that we refuse to accept things and people as they really are. Such acceptance does not mean that we merely give up our previous views, admit defeat, forgo fresh undertakings and cancel ambition; it means that we include in the sphere of our ambition the objective facts of existence and realize that there are things whose alteration is not desirable. We shall in this way give a fresh interpretation to our position in the world, not in the world of our dreams, but in the world of experience and reason; or, from a religious point of view, not in the unreal world of popular hagiography, of the months of Mary and St. Joseph, but in the world of faith with its supernatural enlightenment, its certainties that have been tested in prayer and through the experience of the cross. We shall learn the true value of things and of ourselves; that value will still be considerable and attractive, and it will also be more real.

This is the time, too, when we should practice detachment and purify our motives. Not that we should lose our zest for things or for life; we are still, and we may long remain, at an age of much possible achievement. To be detached is not to retreat from action; it is to stand back in order to gain a clearer view of things. Humanly speaking, it is an act of criticism and realism; in the moral and religious sphere it is a purification; that is, a reassertion of our fidelity that goes deeper than the comfort of its external attraction. St. Térèsa of Lisieux relates that when she was saddened by the sight of the chestnut trees being cut down in the garden she reflected: Had this happened in some other convent, I should not have been so troubled. When St. John the Baptist saw that Jesus was also baptizing and that everyone was now flocking to him, he said, "No one can receive anything except what is given him from heaven. You yourselves bear me witness, that I said, I am not the Christ, but I have been sent before him. He who has the bride is the bridegroom; the friend of the bridegroom, who stands and hears him, rejoices greatly at the bridegroom's voice; therefore this joy of mine is now full. He must increase, but I must decrease" (John 3:27–30). This is the detachment that purifies and brings a sense of reality. It is a proper accompaniment to a man's maturity; negatively, it marks the period of crisis we have described above; positively, it represents the acquirement of a power of objective criticism, of an objective understanding of the world and of oneself, of a critical estimate of one's own life, of deliverance from that obsession with self that often blocks the view of truth.

This return to humility, that is, to truth, provides the possibility of a very genuine religious awareness. If a man who is proud of his ability and somewhat intoxicated by his achievements agrees to take this path, he may learn to rectify his life in the way of faith and to serve God with a deeper love and fidelity. It will be an encounter between the cross and purgatory — an expression without romantic overtones if it is true that purgatory, after the death of the body, is a progressive throwing overboard of such earthly contents of our luggage as prevents us from finding God.

This trial of middle age is eased by the experience of maturity. The worth of things is understood and the states of mind that have real significance, the significance of standing faithfully at one's post without distinction, of being silent, of really doing one's job, even of being misunderstood; the importance, the greatness, of little things, of realities that may not glitter but abide. What is worthwhile seems less exciting, and yet clearer and more enduring. It may be that this was Tauler's[5] reason for asserting that the acquisition of interior peace is not possible before forty, nor of the mystical life before fifty. Of course this situation should be sustained — it would be an immense help if it were — by Christian teaching that is equally real, broad, and critically true. In religion, general and somewhat romantic views may be permissible at the start, but as time goes on there should be no less concern to acquire adult definitions; for example, as regards the relationship between faith and the world, the world that has become known to us as we grow up through its sciences, its work, through the activities of citizenship or political life; or as regards the relationship between interior freedom or the spiritual life, on the one hand, and bodily determinism, the weight of heredity, etc. on the other (it is not possible to be confined forever within the edifying but puerile boundaries of a hagiography that ignores physical and psychological realities, realities, incidentally, which if despised are apt to take their revenge); or finally, as regards the relationship between freedom and authority, and of the lawful position of freedom in the Church. If we ask why the works of Carrel,[6] Lecomte du Nouy,[7] and Teilhard de Chardin,[8] so defective in many respects, have met with such success, is it not because they discuss the spiritual life in terms of adult experience, in relation to the facts of medicine, history, paleontology, natural science? There is a

---

5. Johann Tauler (1300–1361), Dominican friar, mystic, and bishop of Strasbourg.

6. Alexis Carrel (1873–1944), physician, author, and winner of the 1912 Nobel prize for medicine.

7. Pierre Lecomte de Noüy (1883–1947), biophysicist and philosopher.

8. Pierre Teilhard de Chardin (1881–1955), French Jesuit priest, mystic, and paleontologist. He was silenced by Church authorities for his efforts to reconcile Christian theology and evolution.

general feeling that what we need is an authentic and enlightened spirituality in which the absolute is seen to be all the more absolute because of its insertion in the relativity of history and life. Our preaching is often criticized as lacking in reality. What is meant is not that it should be less supernatural or more akin to the daily newspaper, but that it should correspond to the real questions and the real needs of men, more in line with the realities of nature and grace, with the world and with the inner life of the spirit. A director of a youth hostel recently remarked that we "give children a catechism for grown-ups, and grown-ups sermons for children."

Here also diagnosis is easy, and the cure more difficult. And yet it is the diagnosis that must initiate the cure. I trust that these brief observations may prove to be for some Christians not in the least a discouragement, but a help toward self-assessment, and that having reached an age when they can take a realistic view of obstacles and possibilities, they may commit themselves more maturely, and with greater authenticity, to the service of that God from whom no secret is hidden.

—FSL 143–54

THE YOUTHFUL HEART

A youthful heart it is a friendly thing, with an irresistible power of attraction. We can all recognize it and point it out. But we have probably never thought of defining it, and it may be salutary to make the attempt. There is youthfulness of years, bodily youth, and there is also youth of soul. These are not identical (one can be a little old man at twenty or, on the other hand, retain a youthful soul forever). There is, of course, a resemblance; the same word denotes them both. The epithet "young" seems applicable to those who in spirit possess the characteristics of the young in years. What is this latter youthfulness?

It is something flexible and robust, something fresh and thriving; life in abundance, overflowing life. Consider nature in the spring: a young plant, a young animal, is a living being whose reserves of life have not been drawn on, but are fluid and ascending and eager to spend themselves. Primarily, youth means this abundance and exuberance of life's energies. Its outward signs show a particular brilliancy, games are freely played with agility, singing preferred to speech, running to walking. An inner vitality seems to demand an outlet. The same idea seems to be true of youthful institutions: their fullness of life controls their form; their material elements are still flexible and have not hardened; they are still wholly adaptable and ready to flow into fresh channels.

Youth exists, therefore, wherever there is an unused store of energy, untapped and still increasing. "The most recognizable feature of a young man is the absence of fixed decision. He represents virgin energy untapped for any particular purpose. As yet he has pushed nothing aside, and every direction seems equally attractive."[9]

One of the reasons why, at present, we hear not merely of young men, but of "teenagers," not only of a new generation, but of a proud self-conscious youth, as such, is probably due to the fact that the rising generations seem to be equipped with unprecedented spiritual resources ready to serve causes that everyone realizes are completely new and decisive. Never before has "youth" and "not yet thirty" been so discussed, because there has never been so many spiritual resources for the young to utilize in preparation for the unsettled but decisive tasks which we all realize lie ahead. The young and the under-thirty have never been confronted with so many possibilities, with a tomorrow so loaded with fresh tasks and with the unknown. Youth, indeed, is marked by the possibilities open to it and the events of tomorrow; by implicit disinterestedness

9. François Mauriac, *Le jeune homme* (Paris: Hachette, 1926), 10.

combined with a readiness to adventure, and a sense of commitment. Hence its zest for danger and adventure, its love for original undertakings, for everything which means a fresh start. A young man is one who welcomes anything really new, who is looking for and is directed toward some compelling activity, eagerly striving for something original, struggling in hope toward a better world; the spirit of the springtime and of life ascending.

Why is youth superabundantly alive, tense with expectation? Because it is meant to grow up and be fertile. It has been compared to a flower not merely because it is bright and fresh, but because it is on the way to a fully developed life and promises fertility. Childhood does not contain the brilliant originality which makes adolescence so attractive; on its slender and less robust stalk, buds are only germinal and flowers remote. Real youth presupposes a more immediate hope, not merely toward possibilities, the accent of original energies, but a move toward direct fertility and the most developed and active forms of life. Youth is life ascending with untapped energies to a life that is perfect and fruit bearing.

On the other hand, everything which obstructs, which uses up vital energies, and, in using, specializes and so impoverishes or immobilizes them, is tending toward old age. In an ancient tree the sap's ascent is lower every year, until only a single branch receives the remnant of its vitality. In a worn out institution, with its arteries hardened, its ideal is no longer giving life to its administrative apparatus, but the apparatus is somehow supporting enfeebled convictions. In a declining body that has lost its strength and energy, so settled in a single groove as to be unable to turn to any other without excessive difficulty, the mind becomes mechanized and rusty, slowed down and practically incapable of attending to any new ideas. This is old age in different forms.

It is true that other very worthwhile qualities — easier to enumerate because they are possessions — may have replaced those of youth that cannot be catalogued or given a name. To the spiritual qualities of youth — not yet possessed but belonging to the future, not so much an acquisition as a possibility — new qualities have come into being, the fruits of experience, peace, and contemplation. We should be careful not to underestimate these additional gifts of God, summed up in a fine phrase by René Bazin:[10] "With old age the customary things depart, but God arrives." It is not, however, old age of this stature that we have been discussing. Moreover when it does possess this loftier spiritual quality it shares, *ceteris paribus,* in what we find most attractive in youth: its fresh approach to reality, its openheartedness. But that is a matter of the youthful heart, something independent of youthful years, though closely related to them.

The youthful heart is marked first of all by the spirit of adventure, of joy, by a kind of impetuosity, often even by easily aroused enthusiasm, a carefree confidence, an exuberance that seems to indicate inexhaustible strength. "God of those who sing, O Jesus Christ": with these words Clement of Alexandria concludes his *Pedagogue.*

Then we note a certain lack of prudence and diplomacy, a disregard of obstacles. Youth has little interest in the possible; not that it is unacquainted with reality, but the power of the ideal and of sincerity of heart appears able to accomplish anything and removes the word "impossible" from the dictionary. Since compromise is unknown to them, frankness is one of their notable traits; it is evident in their straightforward look, their open, welcoming faces. They enjoy the high privilege of being able to communicate their convictions and to render them acceptable: they believe that truth has power. They believe that everything is worth sacrificing for truth's sake; they would give up a position in life rather than cast off a friend. They believe in friendship and its values; they believe in love. In time of peace politicians fear these disinterested creatures whose lives have

10. René Bazin (1853–1932), French novelist of provincial life.

not yet been controlled by any political label; they can't get a grip on them.

Most modern men have lost the faculty, but the young can still treat some things as despicable. They are capable of indignation and hatred, and what they consider to be true they serve intensely. It is due to this that they reject so much, a rejection that deserves a smile rather than a rebuke. It is sometimes irritating because they will accept no compromise and take no heed of the actual circumstances or of any accommodation that may be necessary. But even in its excess, youth's openheartedness is a testimony to the absolute nature of truth, to the compelling power of what is right, to what may be called the sacred character of innocence. These are priceless realities.

Youth also despises petty details, conventional attitudes that are safe and involve little expenditure of energy, but are useless for real creativity. Childhood is hardly behind him when a young man begins to take up a personal attitude toward life, and soon conformity and mere tradition lose all power over his behavior. His father comes to feel that although he has not lost the confidence of his son, he is no longer everything to him. The adolescent does not look to his father or to his schoolmaster as his guides to life, but to the give and take and fellowship of his friends who sympathize with his dreams and hopes. He works out a kind of common program or doctrine. He discovers and shares something that would never be accepted if dictated. Or if he does commit himself to a master it will be a master of his own choice whom he believes accepts his own ideals and to whom he attributes youth. It is a spontaneity, more ultimate than the slightest acceptance by his adaptable personality of any conventional attitude that might imply willingness to adopt the worn out customs of his elders.

This is true at least of those who are authentically young. For it is a fact that among those who are less than twenty, many cross from childhood without a break to the serfdom of institutions. It may be that the stern law of standardized work absorbs the best of their youth, stifling initiative, allowing no spare time for intellectual pursuits. Or they may accept without resistance the pitiless and easy fashions of modernity, all the interests, the dreary interests, of the teenage world which are practically the same in Buenos Aires, New York, Paris, or Lisbon. All of them infallibly destroy the young in heart. That youthfulness can be preserved, or rather can be unendingly renewed (for youth cannot be preserved) only by a continuing victory of the spirit over the rigidity of conventional attitudes. Any position taken up through conformity or tradition is regarded as a sign of senility. A youthful soul disregards the security and comfort offered by routine; it is enamored by danger and by decisions that are really its own; it creates, with utter sincerity and spontaneity, its own way of life.

This is not due to a mere spirit of independence and even less to a narcissistic attitude (although youth can become a theme for literary exploitation). For the ultimate truth about the young is their capacity for admiration, attachment, and self-giving. It is this that alone makes sense of their other characteristics: their joyfulness and openheartedness, their contempt for mere conventionality. All this without self-giving is no more capable of making the heart young than good deeds without charity can make a Christian. But whenever self-giving exists, the essence of youth is present.

The ability to wonder and to be enthusiastic are qualities natural to youth. Every youth movement counts on this; they succeed because they demand great things, and the most successful are those which ask for everything. When Christ asked the young man to sell all that he had and to follow him, he was offering him the worthiest opportunity of his youth. Unfortunately, however, he began to balance the impulses of his heart against his bank balance and went away sadly; he had lost what was best in him, his youthful heart.

Youth is life ascending and abounding; it needs to spend and give itself; it hears the call of the absolute, of the total demand, with all its implications of enthusiasm and disinterestedness and chivalrous fidelity. At twenty, death is less important than at fifty. What ultimately makes a youthful heart is the power of believing in an ideal and of surrendering completely to it. Not to be merely an owner without ambition, only interested in enjoying an easy life, but eagerly looking ahead, fascinated by an ideal, mastered by it, allowing it to dictate one's actions, subordinating money and comfort to its demands, this is to be young in heart. Youth — at any age — means the upspringing of new energy seeking an outlet in beauty and fertility. It has no room for the sterile monotony, the placid indifference of those without an ideal, that unhappy privilege of those whom nothing moves, nothing attracts. Youthfulness remains so long as a man does not fall into self-absorption, but still allows his life to be sustained by faith in a better future when the sun will shine more brightly.

The aged soul, on the other hand, turns inward on itself and makes disillusionment a virtue. Enchantment is over; the arteries of the heart and mind harden; nothing new is welcome; there is no accommodation for fresh ideas. Reality has come to mean a dull acceptance of the amenities of life, emptied of every truly generous impulse.

Unfortunately it is not only those of advanced years who join the ranks of the disillusioned. For among the young there are many who find no joy in meeting together to speak of our Lord or their country with childlike spontaneity. These old men of twenty do nothing without some reservation; they are always thinking about what can be got out of it, or what impression they are making, their forehead is always furrowed. Their look has lost its frankness; their lips, lips that can be as revealing as a look, lips that once smiled and welcomed, have now tightened, permitting only "a thin and melancholy gleam." "They find it an effort," says Lavedan,[11] "to remember that they once laughed and ran and climbed trees.... Their cold haughty gaze, darts at a man, takes his measure, clothes and unclothes

11. Henri Lavedan (1859–1940), playwright and member of the Académie Française.

him, and turns away." This disillusionment, reticence, and prudence bear witness to the loss of all power of wondering and self-giving.

We have to admit that all life involves some servitude, some fixation, some ageing. And yet we can escape from these restrictions; we need not confine our soul within the boundaries which our profession or social conformity demand; we may establish ourselves elsewhere, filling our hearts with a spiritual treasure in a realm where "neither moth nor rust can corrupt."

The last word on this matter is this: a soul's youth or age is the age of its heart, and the years of a heart are measured by what it loves. "We are as old as our sins," says Mauriac. "We are spiritual usurers." Intrinsically, a soul is neither young nor old; intrinsically it is outside time, and identically the same at the end of a heavily burdened life as on the morning of its baptism. When I speak of a soul as young or old I am not trying to import chronology into something that is outside time. That is impossible. What I am discussing is the soul as a psychological reality. This demands an explanation. Our actions have their origin in ourselves, and yet they shape us; they dispose us to act this way or that, they create an inclination, a personal way of forming a judgment. And as the result of such judgments and choices and basic preferences — provided they are often enough repeated and fit in with each other — a spirit, a mentality becomes a reality within us. Some of these features inevitably predominate and form our character. These dominant features constitute a soul. We are the makers of this soul, having created it or allowed it to be created by early decisions which we could have modified or controlled.

It is thus that the interests in the foreground of our consciousness, in which our other interests are subordinated, generate in us a spirit, a mentality, a character, a soul. A man devoted to acquiring money has a mercenary soul. A man for whom life means nothing more than the enjoyment of gross and brutal pleasures has a bestial soul. It is even possible to speak of a priestly, apostolic, military, revolutionary soul, by observing the predominant interests and activities of any given individual.

The rule is always the same: external reality bores its way into us and enters our lives. It does so through knowledge and love. The mere knowledge of sensual things does not make a man sensual, but if he loves them, then gradually his soul becomes sensual. The mere knowledge of the evolution of a gentleman does not make a gentleman, but if we make his ideal our own we gradually become one. So, when we describe anyone as young in heart or otherwise, it is these formative factors that determine the answer.

When we give our heart to some reality of this world in order to possess and enjoy it, we cease to be children, poorly equipped and unattached, eager to develop, able to offer ourselves for any purpose, and to offer our whole being for that purpose; we cease to be generally serviceable, an ascending and joyful energy. We become involved, attached; the reality we sense holds us and forms us in its image. It contains the moth and rust that invade our treasure and corrode it.

This does not imply any Manichean deviation, any false asceticism. But there can be no doubt that there are things in this world that provide the most intense satisfaction and yet clog our soul and end its youth; how many human lives, for instance, are dwarfed by the lust for gain and pleasure. Let us not deceive ourselves: these things seduce; they seem to offer unending possibilities, and this gives the illusion of life and growth. But it is not really the soul that is renewed; on the contrary, as one activity follows another, as collectively they become more engrossing, as numbers become the only things that matter, as pleasure becomes increasingly repetitive and recondite, the soul becomes proportionately emptier, and any new and genuinely youthful effort is a rare event and a feeble one at that. The youthful heart has no more deadly enemy than these possessive attitudes or these pleasures; they stifle every generous impulse and reduce our immortal soul to contentment with a scrap of soil.

Even spiritual realities cannot prevent us from ageing if we set ourselves up as their masters. They could keep us young, they could maintain a spirit of enquiry in us, but they may also distort us, twisting us into respectable teachers, revered masters, or scholars of renown.

The adversary lurking for a youthful heart is the verb "to have." Youth is poor and knows it. From its point of view everything that tends to make a man an owner decreases his stature. And it is surely true that ownership does work against the youthful spirit, against its carefree joy, its contempt for mere routine and the compromises that make life easy, its willing devotion and disinterested self-giving. I have become a self-satisfied owner of mediocre trivialities, and I have lost youth's essential aptitude; the power to welcome great ideals that can command a lifetime's service.

Ideals, yes, but is it not true that there is only one ideal, the living God, that can perennially rejuvenate our youthful energy? Is it not also true that it is the saints alone who have made every aspect of the youthful heart a practical reality? It is those hidden depths that we must explore if we are to find the phoenix of perpetual youth. St. Augustine of the burning heart has the phrase we need: "Young men, if you would remain young, seek Christ." —FSL 155–63

5

Congar and the Holy Spirit

Congar's last major work, and perhaps his greatest, is the three-volume work I Believe in the Holy Spirit *(1979–80), though he subsequently published two other books on the same topic in 1983 and 1984 (*Esprit de l'homme, Esprit de Dieu, *and* The Word and the Spirit*). It is, however, fair to say that the role of the Spirit was ever-present in his ecclesiological and ecumenical work. This was very evident in the first of the three essays that form* Laity, Church and World *(1960), where Congar wrote much less technically about these issues. This essay, "Holy Spirit and Spirit of Freedom," raises the question, "what does the Spirit mean to Christian life in the world," in addition to the more commonly asked question about the role of the Spirit in the Church. In the world, argues Congar, there are threats to freedom and there is a need to escape at times from the stresses of daily life, but there is more than these two extremes.*

It is absolutely necessary that men should find, in an inner life and the deepest convictions of conscience, means to save their own manhood and that of others.

Faith always makes persons. A religious faith prevents, for example, a worker from being wholly and only a paid "hand," dedicated solely to his work and to the proletarian cause; but this is not so much because such a faith may lead to bourgeois or conventional ideas with regard to established authority. Christianity does not prevent him from being a worker or from being active on behalf of workers' interests. But it does make *impossible* that process of reduction, which Marxism exacts and brings about, from man to worker or a means of production, and from worker to proletarian, fully mobilized for service in its class war. Accordingly, though they are not on the same level with it, faith and a religious life are opposed to Marxism: not only doctrinally, in their positive teaching, but in their attitude toward man and what sort of a creature he is. In the same way, though it is not *of* this world, the Christian religion is a power *in* the world. There is an outstanding opportunity for Christians in this age, one of whose greater problems, greater every day, is to harmonize planning with the individual's nature and rights, the social organization of life with the building up and development of persons. But to cope with that, Christians have got to go back to their first principles.

We have got to be very careful, too, that in acquiring depth and an inner self through religion and spiritual life, we do not cut ourselves off from the world. It cannot be denied that there are dangers here: it is a common reproach to us Christians that we selfishly withdraw into a cozy shelter provided by "spiritual" absorption in the needs of our dear little souls. However liberated we may be from the restrictions imposed by a mechanized world, we are still "in the world," with a part to play in its life and history. As Christians, what we need is not *less* spirituality, but more and more of it, and above all a biblical, that is a genuinely Christian, spirituality. —LCW 10–11

Congar identifies three principal ideas of freedom current in today's world — that which comes from Rousseau, the Marxist idea, and the Stoic idea — and proceeds to distinguish the Christian idea from all three.

Like Stoicism, but to a far greater degree, Christianity refuses to reduce freedom to a matter of free will, the ability to do this or that, the freedom of unconcernedness, or to a liberation from external constraint. Rather it is a spiritual quality of human existence, a perfection or characteristic of man in himself; and, as it actually exists in this or that person, there can be different degrees of it....

Freedom, then, is not simply freedom from whatever prevents me from ploughing my own furrow in my own way without interference: it is, positively, a matter of our ability to share in goodness and truth. It is, indeed, always a question of man's return to himself, but here man has a pattern that is both above and within himself: to return to self is to return to the image of God. To be rid of some external compulsion is only one degree of freedom, and not the highest. The truth is that man could never be more free than were he, by some blessed impossibility, to reach the state of being unable to sin—like God and, in the created order, Christ.

The highest degree of freedom is not to govern oneself, but to be wholly governed by God: not forgetting that, while God is outside and above us, he also dwells within us. Because he is God, he is in some sense within us physically; spiritually and morally he is within us through the free gift of his Holy Spirit "in our hearts" (Gal. 4:6). Thus it is *from within*, gently, that he moves us toward what is good, to the true good. The pressure or attraction under whose influence we act is the Holy Spirit himself. Here the whole subject of Christian freedom is involved; and that would entail discussion of the whole "program" of Christian life and the Christian ethic as a *paschal*, an Easter program, concerned with the achievement of spiritual freedom....

Accordingly, Christian freedom consists in the perfect agreement, not of an "apathetic" will with nature, but of a love-intoxicated will with the saving will of God as it is shown forth in Jesus Christ. "Philip, whoever has seen me, has seen the Father...I am the way" (John 14:9, 6)....Now this will of

God, in action as we see it in Jesus our way, is love and service, the humble service of love; it is love coming into this world to take its evil on itself and to overcome it in the manner of the Suffering Servant: it is what St. Paul calls "the wisdom of the Cross."

—LCW 13–15

In his huge work on the role of the Holy Spirit Congar explores literally every aspect of the question. Here we see him addressing the issue of how the Holy Spirit ensures that the Church will remain faithful to the apostolic faith.

The Church gives its faith to the Word of God, to which the inspired Scriptures bear witness. Throughout the centuries, the Church's life has been a meditation on the Scriptures. The need for the Scriptures to be read in the same spirit and through the same Spirit under whose influence they were written has been stressed again and again in the history of Christianity. The only really adequate way of reading and interpreting Scripture is to do so subject to the movement of the Spirit. Scripture is one of those places where the close connection that exists between the Spirit and the Word, the Paraclete and Christ, is revealed. The whole of Scripture speaks of Christ. This deep meaning of Scripture, however, is disclosed only when we are converted to the Lord, who acts in us as the Spirit (see 2 Cor. 3:16–18). Origen was sometimes excessively subtle in his interpretations of Scripture, but he brought to the study of the Bible something more than a perspicacious spirit. With a heart in which the Spirit of Jesus dwelt, he read the whole of the Christian mystery in the sacred books.

I have used the words "Christian mystery." Christ is the principle and the center of that mystery, but he came "for us men and for our salvation" and he does not operate without Christians, not even without all who are called (see Rom. 8:28–30). This is what enables us to read Scripture "spiritually." In other words, a "spiritual" reading of Scripture is what is done in the communion of the Church and the Holy Spirit. By inspiring Scripture and by throwing light on believers' reading of it, the

Spirit is simply making sure that the text will be without error and those who read it will be orthodox.

This, of course, is a reduction of the part played by the Spirit in the understanding of Scripture. Such a reduction may have been sufficient at a time when the Church was adopting a tight and rather narrow defensive posture against Higher Criticism. Progress in the study of biblical and patristic sources has now made it possible for us to have a much wider view. The Christian mystery is God's revelation and communication of himself through his Son, Jesus Christ, in the Holy Spirit, who is undoubtedly, in the words of Irenaeus of Lyons, the "*communion* with Christ." This is the "spiritual sense" of Origen and the Church Fathers. It is also what the Second Vatican Council meant when it dealt with the question: How to interpret Scripture. The Council fully recognized the historical, cultural, and human conditioning of the sacred texts, their literary genres and so on. It also regarded Scripture to some extent as a sacrament, like the Church itself and, by analogy, the incarnation. It then claimed, "since holy Scripture must be read and interpreted according to the same Spirit by whom it was written," that "no less serious attention must be given to the content and *unity of the whole of Scripture*" and that *"the living tradition of the whole Church* must be taken into account along with the harmony which exists between elements of the faith."

If Scripture is, as far as its content is concerned, the communication of the mystery of Christ, which is the work of the Holy Spirit, then it is clear how, given the necessary assumptions, the Church's Tradition, the Eucharist, and even the Church itself have become assimilated to it, since, because of the activity of the same Spirit, the content is fundamentally the same. This is not simply the teaching of Origen or St. Ambrose. It also forms part of a realistic, yet spiritual view of what is involved. It can also be explained on the basis of John 6 or that of the traditional theme, which was taken up again by Vatican II, of the two tables — the table of the Word and that of the sacrament. Both tables are Christ given to us so that we shall live, and this requires the activity of the Holy Spirit. Each of these realities has an external aspect, which it is possible to consider alone. It is possible to see nothing in Scripture but a literary text, nothing in Tradition but a human history, nothing in the Eucharist but a ceremony and nothing in the Church but a sociological phenomenon. Each, however, also has a deep spiritual aspect, to which God is committed through his Spirit.

The Spirit makes the Word present, taking the letter of Scripture as the point of departure. He enables the Word to speak to each generation, in every cultural environment, and in all kinds of circumstances. He helps the Christian community at different times and in different places to understand its meaning. Is this not what Jesus promised? Did the first witnesses and the first Christian Churches not experience this? Has the Church not always been aware of this and affirmed this when it has spoken about its Tradition? Is it not a point of wide ecumenical agreement today? At certain periods during the history of the Church, notably during the Counter-Reformation and the Catholic restoration after the French Revolution, theologians have especially stressed the guarantee that the Spirit gives to the Church and have interpreted the Church in terms of authority and the magisterium, a guarantee that it cannot err in its teaching. Although I would not wish to overlook this aspect, I would prefer to stress here the part played by the Spirit in making knowledge present in continuity with what has gone before, and to insist on the fact that the whole Christian community, including its pastors, are helped by the Spirit. "You are not to be called 'rabbi,' for you have one teacher and you are all brethren" (Matt. 23:8). The teaching of the Second Vatican Council here is very firm:

> The holy people of God shares also in Christ's prophetic office. It spreads abroad a living witness to him, especially by means of a life of faith and charity.... The body of the faithful as a whole, anointed as they are by the Holy One (cf. John 2:20, 27), cannot err in matters of

> belief. Thanks to a supernatural sense of faith which characterizes the people as a whole, it manifests this unerring quality when, "from the bishops down to the last member of the laity" (Augustine), it shows universal agreement in matter of faith and morals. For, by this sense of faith which is aroused and sustained by the Spirit of truth, God's people . . . clings without fail to the faith delivered to the saints (cf. Jude 3), it penetrates it more deeply by accurate insights and applies it more thoroughly to life.

Congar next turns to the question of how the Spirit continues to work in history today.

This brings us at once to the question: Does he still speak through the prophets? Who would dare to say that he does not? But, if he does, who is it who prophesies? One reply to this question is that the proposal of an objective revelation or the communication of the Word implies a corresponding "spirit of revelation" in the subjects who are to receive it. Because of this, God is constantly active revealing himself in men who are called to believe or who are living by faith. It is, however, necessary to go further than this and ask whether God does not speak today in events and in the lives of men. This is certainly a question that modern man asks again and again.

Inner inspirations and even what John of the Cross called "substantial words," which, in the course of a fervent spiritual life, bring about what they say, such as "Walk in my presence" or "Be at peace," have always been recognized in Christianity. Private revelations have also played a part in the history of the Church. It has long been thought that the lives of the saints form a commentary in action on the Scriptures, and Pope Pius XII went so far as to say, in connection with Thérèse of Lisieux,[1] that the lives of the saints were God's words. It has

1. St. Thérèse of Lisieux (1873–97), a French Carmelite nun who achieved great posthumous fame and influence through the publication of her autobiography, *The Story of a Soul.*

also always been believed that, as the Church is guided by the Holy Spirit in its life, the Church's way of acting, the *usus Ecclesiae,* was a very precious "theological locus," especially sacramentally. Thomas Aquinas often referred to this. The sense of faith, or *sensus fidei* — the term *sensus fidelium* is often used, less precisely, to point to the feeling of Christians themselves — can also be included among the "theological loci." God also makes certain aspects of faith known to this *sensus.*

— HS I, 27–29

In the third volume of the work on the Holy Spirit there is a series of theological reflections, one of the more surprising of which is Congar's exploration of the femininity of the Holy Spirit, all the more surprising, of course, because of his consistent reference throughout the book to the Spirit as "he."

The question of the femininity present in God, or even of the femininity of God, is raised insistently nowadays, in reaction to an overwhelming, centuries-long, male dominance. In every language, the word for God is masculine. In triadology we always speak of his "Son." The Word was made flesh — in the masculine form.

These are, of course, indisputable facts, but one will not insist on them too much if it is remembered how careful the canonical Scriptures are to avoid attributing sex to God. Israel was surrounded by religions with female deities, but there was no goddess alongside the one living God in its own belief and practice. In obedience to his word and to the revelation of Jesus Christ, we call God "Father" but this does not mean that he has a female partner, a bride or mother, alongside him. If we were not afraid of anthropomorphism, we would say, together with Bérulle,[2] that, in the begetting of the Word, God "performed the functions of father and mother, begetting him in himself

2. Pierre de Bérulle (1575–1629), cardinal statesman, mystic, and founder of the French congregation of the Oratory.

and bearing him in his womb." Thomas Aquinas observed that Scripture attributed to the Father, in begetting the Word, what, in the material world, belonged separately to a father and a mother, but that there was no reason in this case to speak of a mother in God because he was pure Act, whereas in the process of begetting, the mother represents what receives passively — this is, of course, an idea no longer acceptable to modern physiology. The Word of God remains.

On the other hand, however, "God created man in his own image, in the image of God he created him, male and female he created them" (Gen. 1:27). If this is true, then there must be in God, in a transcendent form, something that corresponds to masculinity and something that corresponds to femininity.

In fact, there is no lack of feminine characteristics in the God of the biblical revelation, and these are emphasized by the vocabulary of Scripture itself. In the first place, there is the theme of tenderness. This is, of course, not a uniquely feminine attribute: there is a paternal tenderness, and, in Scripture, God, as father, is tender (see Ps. 103:13; Isa. 63:16). Sometimes tenderness is attributed simply to Yahweh (see Ps. 25:6; 116:5; Exod. 34:6). It is, however, indisputably feminine in many of the texts of the prophets and especially in the very concrete image incorporated into the term itself:

> When Israel was a child, I loved him and out of Egypt I called my son.... Yet it was I who taught Ephraim to walk, I took them in my arms, but they did not know that I healed them. I led them with cords of compassion, with the bands of love.... How can I give you up, O Ephraim! How can I hand you over, O Israel!... My heart recoils within me, my compassion grows warm and tender.
>
> (Hos. 11:1–4, 8)

> Is Ephraim my dear son? Is he my darling child? For as often as I speak against him, I remember him still. Therefore my heart yearns for him; I will surely have mercy on him. (Jer. 31:20)

> But Zion said: "Yahweh has abandoned me, the Lord has forgotten me." Can a woman forget her sucking child, that she should have no compassion on the son of her womb?
> (Isa. 49:14–15)

> As one whom his mother comforts, I will comfort you.
> (Isa. 66:13)

The word used in Hebrew for "tenderness" is *rahamim,* "bowels," "entrails," which is the plural of *rehem (raham),* "womb," matrix. Tenderness, then, is feminine. God has the disposition and the love of a mother. Jesus had the same disposition — he is often shown in the Gospels as [literally translated] "moved in his bowels." Feminine qualities, activities, and attitudes, such as feeding with milk, gentleness, love, and so on, are celebrated in Christ, giving rise to the devotion to "Christ our Mother." This was especially an ideal for the superior of a monastic community: the abbot, the father, should be maternal. This ideal was followed in detail by the great abbots and Cistercian monks of the twelfth century — Bernard, Aelred of Rievaulx, Guerric of Igny, Isaac of Stella, Adam of Perseigne, Helinand of Froidmont, and William of Saint-Thierry. These are, however, psychological attitudes rather than theology. The Holy Spirit is not mentioned at all in the monastic texts in this context. The idea of maternity in God does recur in a somewhat curious form in the writings of the English mystic Julian of Norwich, at the beginning of the fifteenth century. She saw three attributes in the Trinity: fatherhood, motherhood, and lordship. It is, however, rather the theme of wisdom that she relies on in attributing motherhood to the second Person.

Wisdom is, as the *sekinah,* Presence or Indwelling of God, a mode of being or action on the part of God and especially with reference to the world, to men, and to Israel. It is a feminine attribute, and it is loved and sought like a woman (Sir. 14:22ff.). Wisdom is a bride and a mother (Sir. 14:26ff.; 15:2ff.). She is the source of fertility, intimacy, and joy. In the

New Testament and theological tradition, Wisdom is appropriated to the Word, Christ. In the Old Testament, on the other hand, Wisdom is often identified with the Spirit (Wisd. 9:17) and many of the ante-Nicene Fathers thought of it as representing the Holy Spirit....

In Christian reflection, the feminine character of God is ultimately attributed to the Holy Spirit. The fact that the words *rilah* or *ruho* are feminine in Hebrew and Syriac respectively has often been used as evidence of this. We shall see later that this may play a part, but, apart from the fact that the Syriac *meltha,* "word," is also feminine, the word *rilah* is often masculine in both languages; in Syriac, it is always masculine when it refers to the third Person. Furthermore, Jerome noted that "Spirit" is feminine in Hebrew, neuter in Greek and masculine in Latin, and interpreted this as a sign of God's nonsexuality. Nonetheless, it is in the linguistic and cultural domains of Judaism and the Syriac world that the Holy Spirit is most frequently called "mother." In the climate of Judaeo-Christianity, this occurred especially in the *Gospel of the Hebrews* or the *Gospel of the Nazarenes,* which are mentioned by Clement of Alexandria, Origen, and Jerome. In Jerome's quotations, we read of the coming of the Spirit on Jesus at the time of his baptism, with the words: "You are my beloved Son." In the *Odes of Solomon,* which originated in Syria, the Dove-Spirit is compared to the mother of Christ who gives milk, like the breasts of God. Finally, within the framework of Judaeo-Christian Ebionism,[3] Elkesai saw in a vision an immense angel, who gave him a book: "This angel was immense, ninety-six miles high, and was accompanied by a feminine being whose dimensions were of the same scale. The masculine being was the Son of God, the feminine was called the Holy Spirit." In the Syrian liturgy, the Spirit is compared to a merciful mother, and Aphraates, a Syrian writing in Persia about 336–45, said that "the man who does not

3. Early Christian heresy denying the divinity of Jesus, stemming from the Jewish sect of Ebionites, who saw Jesus as Messiah because he kept the Law perfectly.

marry respects God his father and the Holy Spirit his mother, and he has no other love.... " —HS 3, 155–57

It is a fitting conclusion to this little selection of texts that we turn to Congar's writings linking his theology of the Holy Spirit with his ecclesiology. The following selections come from the 1968 English language publication The Revelation of God, *itself part of the larger original French collection,* Les voies du Dieu Vivant *(Paris: Cerf, 1962). The first explicitly discusses the role of the Holy Spirit in the Church.*

The present question...simply concerns the Holy Spirit in the Church. I shall show: (1) that he is given to the Church as such and enables her to have a stable existence in the world as the body of Christ; (2) how he produces in that Church all the activities of her life, and how he is the ultimate activating principle of her unity.

The Holy Spirit was already at work in Israel before Christ: he it was who, working through Moses, had led the people of God out of Egypt and continued to guide them through the judges, the kings, and the prophets (cf. Isa. 63:11–12). And yet it is evident that he was sent in an absolutely new way as the result of the "Passover" of Jesus to his Father (his passion and resurrection; what our Lord, in St. John, calls his "glorification"). Jesus made this abundantly clear; the apostles constantly describe the Spirit of Pentecost as the gift especially accompanying the messianic age; the novelty of this coming was so radical that St. John could write, "For the Spirit was not yet in being, as Jesus had not yet been glorified" (7:39). Thus the same Spirit which led Israel and filled the world (cf. Wisd. 1:7) was communicated at Pentecost under new conditions and new modalities. What were these conditions and modalities?

Under the old dispensation God's Spirit worked through men who had been called to lead the people: priests, kings, and especially prophets. In the messianic or Pentecostal régime he is given to each and all. In the fourteenth to the sixteenth chapters of St. John, Jesus, speaking to the Twelve, who simultaneously represented both the tiny remnant and the first-fruits of the new people of God, said again and again: I will give *you,* I will send to *you,* he will teach *you,* he will guide *you,* he will tell *you.*... In this way he indicated that the Spirit was to be given both to individuals and to the community, to all men as one man, and creating that one man. This is why the Spirit came down upon the apostles and laity who were *assembled together;* he was given at the same time to all and each; he was given to the gathering, to the disciples as a whole — a fact made clear in Acts by the insistent use of the phrase *epi to auto,* all together: 1:15; 2:1, 44, 47. The Spirit requires a certain disposition of unanimity, and at the same time he brings unity into existence. He forms into a single body believers who have been baptized into a single spirit (1 Cor. 12:13); he builds up this body and out of the community of believers makes a temple which all construct together (Eph. 2:18–19).

Under the old dispensation, God's Spirit entered into the leaders of the people, but a new mode of his presence was foretold as the characteristic of the messianic age. He was *to rest* upon the Messiah: Isa. 11:2; 61:1. This was fulfilled in our Head, Jesus Christ, as he himself affirmed (Luke 4:18–21) and as it was made manifest at his baptism (Mark 1:9–11). The prophets had also foretold that, with the coming of the messianic age, the Spirit would be widely diffused and given.

It is this which Jesus promised to fulfill and did in fact fulfill: "I will ask the Father and he will give you another to serve as Advocate and be with you to the end of time" (John 14:16). The terms used in this promise are remarkable. For the messianic community, the Spirit will be a gift, and a gift that will never leave it: he *will be with* the disciples as Jesus had been with them, in order to assist them, and this until the end of the present age, *eis ton aiόna.*

The Fathers had a predilection for these texts and were concerned to explain how the Spirit is the source of all the Church's life, an idea which the Latin Fathers, St. Augustine especially, expressed in the dictum: the Holy Spirit is *the soul of the Church*. Classical theology, papal encyclicals, and contemporary theology of the Church have adopted this idea and given it precision. The Holy Spirit, they affirm, does not enter into composition with the Church in the way the human soul enters into composition with the body; the words "form" or "formal cause" may not be used in this matter, at least not in their technical meaning. We must speak instead of a principle of life in the Church that is transcendent and yet active, dwelling in her, spiritually present in her, polarizing and drawing to himself every element in the Church which is divine. This is indeed the function of a soul, but the expression avoids — and the greatest care must he taken to see that we do avoid—the disastrous error of imagining some physical connection to exist that would transform the Holy Spirit into a single reality with the Church.

We must not even speak of an incarnation.... The Holy Spirit was sent at Pentecost to a Church that was already endowed with her constitution and structure; he comes into her as a principle of life and movement, but the Church exists through being instituted by Jesus Christ. When we examine in the New Testament the special work of the Holy Spirit in relation to the work of salvation, we find that Christ gave to the Church in general and to individuals in particular, an existence in the realm of the new creation; the Holy Spirit was sent to give both of these life and movement, so that they may produce the activities and achievements that befit them. As regards the individual soul, this is made very clear in passages such as Galatians 4:4–6 and Romans 8:15. In like manner, the New Testament speaks of the Holy Spirit as *being given, received, remaining with, indwelling, witnessing, guiding, teaching,* etc. He is a Person who dwells in the Church and acts in her. He is not a mere force or a mere activating principle that becomes a part of her reality.

This explains the fact that whereas the hypostatic union between the word of God and manhood in Jesus makes that manhood sinless and adorable, the coming of the Holy Spirit into the Church as an indwelling and active soul allows what is human and therefore fallible in her to remain, as such, human and fallible. It leaves the Church conditioned by a genuine historical development, a genuine dependence upon the conditions which space and time impose.

What therefore is the nature of the bond that unites the Church with the Holy Spirit? It is, as we have shown elsewhere, a union based upon an alliance, the grounds of which are the most stable, the most holy conceivable, because they are the products of God's will and faithfulness. If we are certain that God is in action in the Christian sacraments or in those deeds of the hierarchy which touch upon the very constitution of the Church, if, for example, wedded Christians can be sure that through the sacrament of marriage they are united in the sight of God and through an act of God himself, if baptism incorporates us with certainty in Jesus Christ, if the consecration in the Eucharist gives us his body, and sacramental absolution his forgiveness, if a solemn definition of a council or of the pope as supreme pastor accurately defines a point of divine revelation, this is because God is faithful to the promise he has personally given to his Church, whose essential constitution is involved to these various actions. It is because he is faithful to his alliance....

This is why the Church through the gift of the Holy Spirit and through his indwelling in her — the supreme factor in the new and conclusive alliance — has a stability and a real infallibility in matters which concern her existence as the New Eve, the Bride of Christ, his helpmate in the work of the second creation, which is that of the redemption and communion between men and God in Jesus Christ. Perhaps the strongest testimonies on this unfailing characteristic of the Church are those which we find in the Fathers or in the writers of the age of persecution: St. Irenaeus, Tertullian, St. Cyprian. We will quote only one passage from Tertullian:

> Very well let us admit it; all of them have been deceived; the apostle was deceived when he bore witness (to this church or that); the Holy Spirit has not kept watch over any of them in order to lead them into truth, that Spirit who had been sent by Christ and who he had asked the Father should be the teacher of truth, the steward of God, the vicar of Christ. He has neglected his duties and has allowed the Churches to take an altered view of the doctrine which he himself taught them through the apostles. But is it, in fact, likely to be true that so many Churches of such importance should have strayed and then finally come to agree in the same belief?

We must add, however, that although the Church is sure of the faithfulness of her Lord and of the Spirit given her as a dowry, she still remains the human aid of the most holy God; she has to imitate Jesus who in his manhood, knowing that his Father unfailingly heard him (John 11:42), prayed whenever he did anything that concerned the Church or involved her existence in the future: before he chose the apostles or when the wind buffeted their ship, before St. Peter's confession of faith, and, with reference to that apostle, for the sending of the Spirit and the unity of believers.

In short, Jesus prayed for the Church. He also prayed during his baptism by John, when he was consecrated for his ministry (Luke 3:21). In her turn the Church must pray that the activity of the Spirit may accompany her preaching of the word, the celebration of the sacraments, the initiative and the decisions of the spiritual authority. She prays "through Jesus Christ." Or, to express this more profoundly: the body, united to its Head, prays with him with one voice, as the Fathers, St. Augustine in particular, are keen to emphasize. Thus the Church must constantly be asking, through her Lord and Bridegroom, that all this work of her self-development and her life may be accomplished, and this she does by accompanying all her actions with an *epiclesis,* that is, an invocation of the Holy Spirit.

Do we priests and preachers think of this when we carry out, even (and especially . . .) with authority, the ministry of the word, the sacraments, or spiritual "government." Let us ask the Spirit to add his witness to our own, as Scripture phrases it: celebrate with us, in the magnificent words of the liturgy of St. John Chrysostom.

As soon as the Spirit is given, he begins to act. This comes out with remarkable clarity with respect to Jesus: immediately he has been consecrated for his messianic ministry, through baptism and the descent of the Spirit, he was driven by the Spirit to perform its first act. A similar activity is observable with regard to the Church: the summary given in a responsory of the liturgy of Pentecost: "They were all filled with the Holy Spirit and (immediately) began to preach" is an accurate expression of the narrative recorded in Acts. As soon as the Holy Spirit had come down the apostles began to speak, the Church took form, began to live and expand. It has been remarked with truth that the whole of this early history could be summarized in the following verse: "The Church throughout Judaea, Galilee and Samaria enjoyed a period of peace . . . and it increased in numbers under the guidance of the Holy Spirit" (9:31). It is equally well summarized in another verse which precisely defines, although very briefly, the elements of the Church's internal life: "They devoted themselves in close fellowship to instruction from the apostles, to regular Breaking of Bread and to prayer" (2:42). In this verse we discover the three spheres of activity which form the norm and provide the means of the Church's self-development: teaching (the *magisterium),* the liturgy with its two elements, sacrifice and prayer (priesthood), community life regulated by pastoral authority (the rule of law). This is the framework within which the Church's life has developed from the beginning. It will serve to bring our thoughts on the way the Spirit acts in that life into order.

We would first point out an essential feature of that action that is illustrated by the relationship between the two verses quoted above (remembering that there is other evidence): the

Church develops through a combination of the external action of the Holy Spirit and the external action of the apostolic authority. This is also made clear by the teaching of the encyclical *Mystici Corporis* (June 29, 1943): the Church, it affirms, is the product of two "missions," both of them harmonious and both divine: a "spiritual" mission and a "juridical" mission, that of the apostolate which is continued in the various kinds of ministerial action that flow from apostolic authority. We shall not now discuss the research that has been carried out on the foundations of these ideas in Scripture . . . but simply note the three conclusions that result from it: (1) Jesus employed and sent two agents to do *his* work, *his* Spirit and *his* apostles. (2) These two agents *act in unison* in their *mutual* work of building up the Body of Christ. (3) Nevertheless the Spirit retains a kind *of freedom* or autonomy.

The brief comments given below refer not so much to the origins of the Church as to her later, postapostolic history. They presuppose these origins and are sanctioned by them, just as the apostolic period which in its essential elements has always been for her, *de jure* and *de facto,* a normative reference.

—RG, 148–55

LIFE IN THE CHURCH: TEACHING

One of the activities most explicitly attributed to the Holy Spirit is that of *testifying,* or, in biblical phraseology, doing the work of God in the sphere of faith and knowledge. Jesus himself also attributes to the Spirit the work of *teaching*. His way of expressing this is most noteworthy: "I have said these things to you while still with you. But the Advocate, the Holy Spirit, whom the Father will send in my name, will teach you everything and recall to your minds all that I have said to you . . . I have much more to tell you, but you could not bear it now. But when he comes, the Spirit of truth, he will lead you into all the truth. For what he tells you will not be his own, but all that he has heard.

And he will tell you of the things to come. He will enhance my glory; for he will he enriched from what is mine and pass it on to you" (John 14:25–26; 16:12–14).

These words express, with great precision, two aspects of that activity of the Holy Spirit, two different but related and basically complementary aspects. On the one hand, the Paraclete (Assistant) only brings to mind what Jesus has said: he will he enriched by *that.* On the other, he is to teach "everything"; he will, lead men into "all the truth"; he will declare it and even tell them "of the things to come." In short, he will unfold the truths of salvation more extensively than Jesus did. We are clearly confronted here by two functions of truth and of the Master who teaches it: a function related to its source, which remains a constant norm, and a function related to its unfolding, which takes place in successive stages. All this, in my opinion, should he envisaged in the setting of the great biblical idea of Christ considered as simultaneously our Alpha and our Omega. Jesus Christ is the source of all things, the originating principle of the new creation, the creation that comes into being through salvation and grace. But he must "come to his fullness" in us (Eph. 1:23), achieve his perfect stature through us, and develop until he is utterly complete (4:13, 15), and this not only as regards grace and charity, but also as regards knowledge.

This is basically what is meant by Tradition, of which, as the profoundest theology affirms, the originating principle is the Holy Spirit. For Tradition involves both continuity and development; in the here and now it involves a reference to both the beginning and the end. The sacraments involve this also, and theology analyzes the threefold relationship of their symbolism with the salvation achieved by the Lord's Passover, with grace at the present time and with that future glory whose initial stage they contain.

The facts, moreover, show that in the Church's tradition, from the beginning down to our days, there is both identity in transmission and increase in knowledge. St. John, who, in comparison with the earlier Gospels, gives a more profound view of

Christ, remarks several times that the apostles had not understood this or that saying or action of the Lord. They realized their meaning later, thanks to the Spirit of Pentecost. What was thus accomplished within the space of a generation, and with the guarantee of God's grace of revelation, has been continued in a certain way throughout the ages and with the assistance of the Holy Spirit. And just as the apostolic body effected externally and visibly what the Holy Spirit effected internally and in a hidden manner, so these two aspects of testimony reappear in the teaching activity of the Church, of whom the first Vatican Council says that she has received the doctrine of faith "as a deposit to be faithfully kept and infallibly declared."

We cannot, in these pages, even give an outline of a theory of Tradition or of dogmatic development, nor even a theology of the *magisterium*. But we must complete our brief comment with a remark of considerable importance. The Holy Spirit is not given to the Church exactly as he was given to the prophets and the apostles. To these he was given in order that the foundations of the Church might be established, to bestow her belief upon her through a special grace of revelation. But the foundations were established once for all time.... The grace given to the Church is not the grace of new revelation, but of permanency in the faith of the apostles and of exact definition of the faith which cannot remain in her inert and sterile. The accepted theological word is that of assistance, and the phrase used in our treatises in the infallibility of the pope himself is that he is assisted "lest he err," in such a way that when he makes a judgment that implicates the Church as a whole, in that supreme act he cannot be deceived. This does not dispose of his obligation (also incumbent on the Church as a whole) to seek by human endeavor, with the assistance of grace that must be asked for, to ascertain what the truth, tradition, and the "deposit" really are. It follows, therefore, that even in the case of dogmatic definitions, problems concerning the authentic relationship between their general statements and their details with their sources are not eliminated: it is not enough to make a general appeal to the assistance Christ promised to his Church, even though that promise and assistance are the real and objective foundation of the Church's infallibility.

What is meant here by "the Church"? We have deliberately used this general word — incidentally, the word used by the Vatican Council — but we must now give it definition. We would, in any case, ask that whenever this word is encountered, its content, its coverage ... should be examined. Does it designate the hierarchy alone, or the laity alone, or does it include them both? The answer rings out clearly: it includes them both, organically united in a single body. This is undoubtedly the traditional position. It may be expressed in the following way: the Holy Spirit is given to the entire body, and he gives life to all the members of the body, to each member according to his nature and function. Some are simple living cells in the body, called into being in order to live; others have received a ministerial function, as St. Paul explains: "Some [Christ] made apostles, some prophets, some evangelists, others he made pastors and teachers. His gifts were made for the perfecting of the saints, for the work of the ministry, for the building up of the body of Christ" (Eph. 4:11–12). These latter are assisted and led by the Holy Spirit so that they may not be simply members (it will be evident in what sense we take this word), but pastors and teachers, overseers (bishops: Acts 20:28), and, finally, a supreme overseer or pastor, with respect to which the capital words recorded by St. John were spoken (John 21:15–17; Luke 22:32; Matt. 16:17–19).

In this organic setting which is, we repeat, that of Tradition (and of the encyclical *Mystici Corporis),* it can easily be seen that *the whole Church* cooperates in guarding and unfolding the deposit of faith, in bearing apostolic witness to it, in intellectual reflection upon it, and, of course, in living from it in prayer and holiness. The entire history of the Church as well as her present circumstances illustrate this truth. It was the pope, the supreme spokesman and pastor of the Church, who defined the dogma of Mary's bodily assumption, but he did not do so without first consulting the bishops and through them their clergy and people. Nor was his action without recognition of the fact that for centuries Christian devotion has understood that Mary, "the eschatological icon of the Church," joined to the incarnate word as his immaculate Mother, had already personally received what is promised as a gift to all Christians at the end. In fact a host of examples could be given in illustration of this truth of the organic quickening of the whole body and of every member in the degree of his membership. —RG 155–59

SACRAMENTAL LIFE AND SANCTIFICATION

We shall simply note the following points, without developing them:

It is the Holy Spirit who operates in the Christian sacraments. No means of sanctification begins to work in the Church without his presence and activity.

The Spirit of Pentecost is always a Spirit of Catholicity; one of the most striking features of Christian holiness is the infinite variety of the type. The Fathers had a predilection for comparing the Holy Spirit's action with that of the rain or the sun from which every created being benefits according to its nature or to that of the mind and nervous system which affects each part of the body according to its function and needs.

The action of the Spirit might also he considered in the different stages of the movement by which he endeavors to lead us from sin to purity of life and perfect communion with God and, in him, with all good things. We might consider the way in which he first makes us realize that we are sinners and moves us to seek forgiveness (cf. John 16:8), then to desire the good and to do penance, then gives us the conviction that the faith is true, and the sense that we are the children of God. We could examine how he enables us to call upon our Father in prayer, and bestows the calm and powerful certainty that we are indeed

God's children, and his unruffled and potent guidance of our lives, and all the consequences of grace in joy and peace. These are realities whose hallowing experience those who pray with faith have undergone and continually undergo.

Now the work done by the Holy Spirit in an individual soul, as though it were the only one in the world, is also done by him in countless souls, harmonizing each and all in the development of a history which, amid the history of the world in general, is a history of holiness in that world and of the world's salvation. While bringing to each man his daily bread of grace, he carries on the construction of a single work: Scripture, speaking of this, not only mentions a city (Jerusalem), but also a temple and a body, metaphors which all imply the ideas of a unity formed from diversity and of a reality which grows by the addition of new elements in accordance with a total plan fixed beforehand. In the New Testament the Holy Spirit is explicitly connected with the descriptions of the temple and the body. Moreover the body and the temple are the same thing, since in the messianic régime of the temple now at last existing, there is no other real temple than the spiritual body of Christ (John 2:19–21). When Jesus gives us his Spirit he sanctifies us and makes us the members of his body; and doing this he fulfils God's purpose — to dwell in his creation that has at last achieved its unity, as in a temple of absolute holiness, *not made by the hand of man,* in the image and like an extension of that body, absolutely holy and pure, which the holy Spirit, and no human eros, formed in the womb of the Virgin Mary: cf. Luke 1:35. — RG 159–60

THE LIFE OF THE CHURCH AS A SOCIETY AND ITS SPIRITUAL GOVERNMENT

We shall be dealing here not with the intimate life of the Church, not with the holiness that belongs to her inner and personal reality, but with what is externally observable in her structure and historical development.

This also concerns the body as a whole. The Church does not exist solely for the clergy, and the laity do not exist as an inactive and inert mass within her. The teaching of the apostles is that the spiritual gifts distributed to all Christians and with which each man "should serve with the particular gift God has given him, as faithful dispensers of the magnificently varied grace of God" (1 Pet. 4:10).

> Men have different gifts, but it is the same Spirit who gives them. There are different ways of serving God, but it is the same Lord who is served. God works through different men in different ways, but it is the same God who achieves his purposes through them all. Each man is given his gift by the Spirit in order that he may serve the common good. One man's gift by the Spirit is to speak with wisdom, another's to speak with knowledge. The same Spirit gives to another man faith. Behind all these gifts is the operation of the same Spirit, who distributes to each individual man, as he will. (1 Cor. 12:4–11)

But, as we have already shown, if the whole body is quickened, it is quickened organically and in such a manner that some members exercise a regulating power with the precise purpose of serving unity. Chapters 12–14 of the first epistle to the Corinthians show how St. Paul understood these matters; the pastoral epistles and several passages of the Acts show that in the Church there exist functions of pastoral authority derived from those of the apostles, whose permanent responsibility it is, among other things, to regulate the activity of the laity with reference to the unity that must be maintained. Consequently, under the action of one and the same Spirit the life of the Church always exhibits itself as involving a kind of polarity between an abundance of individual initiative and moderating control, between a great variety of gifts or contributions and firm declarations of the requirements of unity.

The diversity of gifts is the reason for the diversity of vocations and tasks. For, from a Christian point of view, all men, and more especially all believers, form a single body in which ability and potentiality of a given individual represents, as such, a vocation and a service. Within the body all activity is the expression of tasks being done and responsibility accepted in view of a collective work whose main lines we know, but whose details form part of that "daily bread" which we ask God each day to give us and make known to us. The particular task of a given individual becomes his vocation from the fact that he receives it from God as his special work within his general vocation as a member of Christ. This task is determined by his gifts, and among these the attractions or the idea of some reality is not the least significant. It is determined also by circumstances or events, these masters whom God appoints. Thus the slightest initiative suggested to us by the Holy Spirit, the services to others to which he prompts us, the tasks he moves us to accept, count not only as a means of fulfilling our own destiny (cf. Eph. 2:10), but also for the building up of the body of Christ and for the coming of his kingdom.

When an attraction to some work or to some service has been unmistakably felt to concern the body of Christ and his kingdom, and instead of remaining exclusively inward and personal seeks expression in some corporate body or activity of the Church and receives the sanction of the spiritual authority, then we may speak of a vocation in a stronger and more definite sense: vocation to the priesthood, to the monastic life (with its many spheres of charity), and including the vocation to the lay apostolate in authorized Catholic Action. It is always the Holy Spirit who directs matters to the extent in which the fidelity of some or the fervor of others permits him. He aims at making the laity realize the nature of their work of service and enables them to carry it out; and he inspires the pastors who are responsible for harmonizing the general development of the body and for the factors necessary for its unity.

Such is the law of the Spirit's action in the ordinary course of our lives and in the environment of the humblest parish. Transposed, it is equally applicable to the history and development of the Church as a whole. For the Church does develop; although she is not of the world, she is in it and has a mission to it. She cannot disregard the world's development and its needs, first because she must herself exist in its midst, and secondly because she must supply an answer to its needs and thereby fulfill the commission given to her to proclaim the Good News to all creation (Mark 16:15). But the world is not inert; it does not stay motionless, waiting for a word to drop out of eternity. The centuries advance, mankind increases, new fields of activity are endlessly opened up or disclosed. If the Church is alive and fruitful, if she is to have a message and a special love for everything which comes into existence throughout space and time, if the Spirit is that living water in her that was promised by Jesus, and that, as it streams along, endlessly renews the foliage of the living trees whose leaves, according to the Apocalypse (22:1–2), serve for the healing of the nations, then, just as the sap rises up into the branches, producing a constant succession of leaves, flowers, and fruit, so the Spirit is constantly creating initiatives of every kind, every sort of activity and movement. At this point we must inevitably refer to the famous passage from St. Irenaeus (c. 180) on the faith which always remains identical with that of the Apostles, and yet is always alive, and "which always, under the action of the Spirit, is like a precious liquid kept in a vessel of good quality that rejuvenates itself and even rejuvenates the vessel that contains it. . . . For where the Church is, there also is the Spirit of God, and where the Spirit of God is, there the Church is and every grace."

These noble themes, whose realism should not be obscured by their metaphorical expression, have been constantly verified in the history of the Church, especially in missionary enterprises and those of the apostolate. When, for example, I read the scrolls that flanked the altar of the Missionary Pavilion in the colonial Exhibition of 1931 I was almost physically affected; nothing could have been more eloquent than that sober list of new races evangelized, of martyrs, of the religious orders devoted to missions. If we take a closer look at this question and study, for example, the missionary endeavor of the nineteenth century, the Spirit's activity becomes obvious; in the words of Pius XI, we are taking part in a continuation of Pentecost and of the Acts of the Apostles. We constantly come across inner callings as definite as those heard by St. Paul.... We see almost every year new missionary orders coming into existence, often in improbable circumstances and marked by the suffering of the cross. The active participation of women in this movement took place a century before that of our own time when women have come to take their part in university, professional, and political life.... In all this two elements are especially noteworthy with regard to the action of the Spirit in the Church.

First, we note the fact of an adaptation of which no one, at the start, had any idea, or of an astonishing concurrence of men and circumstances that had been neither expected nor foreseen. When St. Paul on the road to Damascus suddenly received the manifestation of the Lord Jesus, a disciple, Ananias, who had never seen Paul and only knew that he had done considerable harm to the believers in Jerusalem, received a mysterious command to welcome him (Acts 9:10–11). In all the enterprises which God promotes, he causes similar things to happen: the unfailing sign that the Holy Spirit is at work is that people who had not previously known each other, disparate circumstances which no one had prearranged, finally come together in some common activity for the building up of the body of Christ. When, for example, Father Cardijn,[4] a priest in a Brussels suburb, formed the idea that was soon to find expression in the creation of the Young Christian Workers, Pius XI, on his part, was "not without a divine inspiration," forming the idea of Catholic Action, "the participation of the laity in the apostolate of the hierarchy." The two men were to meet, and what

4. Joseph Leo Cardijn (1882–1967), Belgian priest and founder of the Young Christian Workers.

each had created was made more perfect by the contribution of the other.

This fact also provides an illustration of the second feature, connected with what we have said about the organic nature of the Church. The Church's life is symphonic; in it every member has his own theme to contribute, corresponding to his nature, his gifts, and his position in the Church. Or he is like one of the strings whose combined sound the musical instrument expresses. To take an example nearer to present-day experience, Father Godin, describing the creation of the Mission de Paris and of episcopal reactions to it, remarked, "They have their hand on the brake, we are in the driver's seat; both of us are needed." This admirably expresses a characteristic aspect of the way things happen.

The Holy Spirit is a spirit that finds new ways that bring about renewal and adaptation. He is constantly stimulating movements of this kind within the Church; I have discussed this at length in *Vraie et fausse reforme* (Paris: Cerf, 1950). Now in order that these movements of adaptation, renewal or reform may be a genuine movement of *the Church,* they must be harmonized with unity and they must issue from the heart of tradition and not from innovations that are foreign to it. The concrete and practical criterion of concordance with the Church is the approval of the spiritual authority who is the guardian of both tradition and unity. That is why the different movements we have been considering must be developed in a kind of a dialogue between the elements of initiative, which are often on the periphery, with the elements at the center. In reality both these elements fuse into a common work in obedience to the same spirit. It is the same spirit who moves some to seek new ways and others to ensure that there is no straying from tradition and unity, for "if these are lacking, the new way is a mere deviation."

From all this we can see how the Holy Spirit is the conductor of the full orchestra of the Church's life, and the invisible controller of her communion.

Nothing less than the Spirit of God could have the power to bring so many different realities into unity and yet to respect their differences, and this, in fact, is the Spirit's special work. We have seen that he is given to the whole and to every part with regard to that part's function in the whole (for the building up of the body). He is intrinsically a Spirit of Communion. The daily, normal actions of the members, as they mutually show forth Christ, help and fulfill each other, is inspired by him. He also inspires the harmonization of the elements contributed by individuals into the unity and utility of the whole. Thus, *as Spirit* he is the inner law of the Mystical Body, as a whole and in its parts. It is not surprising that St. Thomas considered that the grace of the Spirit is the essential element in the new law, and that tradition has often perceived in the Christian Pentecost, the successor of the Jewish Pentecost, the feast of the gift of the law, the coming of the new law, the communion of the most widely differing members in the same unity. This indeed is the Holy Spirit's special work: to bring plurality and diversity into unity — without violence and by an interior stimulation that acts as a spontaneous and joyful initiative in the individual.

This corresponds with special truth to the personal nature of the Holy Spirit — if "personal nature" is a phrase applicable to him. He is not only love but as the Third Person in the divine Trinitarian reality, the final moment of the fertility, it is his work to continue and in some ways to extend to creation God's fertility; the communication of his inmost being. By his nature he is the communication of a unity to many, who retain their manifold distinction, a unity which these many discover to be their fulfillment and joy. He is essentially Communion. That is why the most profound and comprehensive remark about him is that which concludes the first epistle to the Corinthians: "The grace that comes through our Lord Jesus Christ, the love that is God, and the fellowship [i.e., the communion, the communication] that is ours in the Holy Spirit be with you all!" —RG 161–67

Congar was confined to the hospital for the last ten years of his life. In the conclusion to Bernard Lauret's set of interviews conducted at his bedside, Congar said:

Withdrawn from active life, I am united to the Mystical Body of the Lord Jesus of which I have often spoken. I am united to it, day and night, by the prayer of one who has also known his share of suffering.

I have a keen awareness of the vast dimensions of the Mystical Body. By and in the Holy Spirit I am present to its members, known (to me) and unknown. Ecumenism obviously plays a part in this. It is intercession, consolation, thanksgiving, as the Lord wills. —FYCT, 86–87

MODERN SPIRITUAL MASTERS
Robert Ellsberg, Series Editor

Already published:

Dietrich Bonhoeffer (edited by Robert Coles)
Simone Weil (edited by Eric O. Springsted)
Henri Nouwen (edited by Robert A. Jonas)
Pierre Teilhard de Chardin (edited by Ursula King)
Anthony de Mello (edited by William Dych, S.J.)
Charles de Foucauld (edited by Robert Ellsberg)
Oscar Romero (by Marie Dennis, Rennie Golden, and Scott Wright)
Eberhard Arnold (edited by Johann Christoph Arnold)
Thomas Merton (edited by Christine M. Bochen)
Thich Nhat Hanh (edited by Robert Ellsberg)
Rufus Jones (edited by Kerry Walters)
Mother Teresa (edited by Jean Maalouf)
Edith Stein (edited by John Sullivan, O.C.D.)
John Main (edited by Laurence Freeman)
Mohandas Gandhi (edited by John Dear)
Mother Maria Skobtsova (introduction by Jim Forest)
Evelyn Underhill (edited by Emilie Griffin)
St. Thérèse of Lisieux (edited by Mary Frohlich)
Flannery O'Connor (edited by Robert Ellsberg)
Clarence Jordan (edited by Joyce Hollyday)
G. K. Chesterton (edited by William Griffin)
Alfred Delp, S.J. (introduction by Thomas Merton)
Bede Griffiths (edited by Thomas Matus)
Karl Rahner (edited by Philip Endean)
Sadhu Sundar Singh (edited by Charles E. Moore)
Pedro Arrupe (edited by Kevin F. Burke, S.J.)

Romano Guardini (edited by Robert A. Krieg)
Albert Schweitzer (edited by James Brabazon)
Caryll Houselander (edited by Wendy M. Wright)
Brother Roger of Taizé (edited by Marcello Fidanzio)
Dorothee Soelle (edited by Dianne L. Oliver)
Leo Tolstoy (edited by Charles E. Moore)
Howard Thurman (edited by Luther E. Smith, Jr.)
Swami Abhishiktananda (edited by Shirley du Boulay)
Carlo Carretto (edited by Robert Ellsberg)
John XXIII (edited by Jean Maalouf)
Jean Vanier (edited by Carolyn Whitney-Brown)
The Dalai Lama (edited by Thomas A. Forsthoefel)
Catherine de Hueck Doherty (edited by David Meconi, S.J.)
Dom Helder Camara (edited by Francis McDonagh)
Daniel Berrigan (edited by John Dear)
Etty Hillesum (edited by Annemarie S. Kidder)
Virgilio Elizondo (edited by Timothy Matovina)
Metropolitan Anthony of Sourozh (edited by Gillian Crow)